June Durant is a qualified history teacher and youth leader. She has taught the whole age range from two years to 60 years. Ten of those years in Africa at secondary, tertiary and primary schools; in this country, both in rural middle England and inner city multi-cultural.

The author is widely travelled and always looking for adventure, one of which was sailing around the world in a container ship. From an early age, she has kept a diary or journal. She is a keen genealogist and a member of the Jane Austen Society UK. She lives close by her twin daughters and four grandchildren, their cats, dogs and other animals.

To Phebe and Abigail

My test-pilots during lockdown.

June Durant

SEARCHING FOR WORDS IN JANE AUSTEN

AUSTIN MACAULEY PUBLISHERS™

LONDON • CAMBRIDGE • NEW YORK • SHARJAH

A CIP catalogue record for this title is available from the British Library.

ISBN 9781398448810 (Paperback)
ISBN 9781398448827 (ePub e-book)

www.austinmacauley.com

First Published 2023
Austin Macauley Publishers Ltd®
1 Canada Square
Canary Wharf
London
E14 5AA

Thank you to my daughters, Pippa and Jenny for their technical help and support, and thank you to my best friend, Sue, who never gave up.

The silhouette on the cover is based on Jane Austen's statue in Chawton.

Table of Contents

On each of the succeeding pages, there is a short introduction followed by examples of twenty nouns, proper nouns or other descriptive words to be found in Austen's life, work and her Georgian and Regency world. Beneath that list of twenty are ten sentences and one word from the examples will be found in each.

The following should be noted:

Capital letters and punctuation can be ignored when searching for words. The spelling of towns and cities, sometimes surnames, was fluid and not standardised throughout Austen's writing. Although a Dr Johnson admirer, Miss Austen does not always abide by his dictionary spelling; also, Jane Austen had an idiosyncratic habit of confusing the i before e rule. For example, freindship rather than friendship, greive instead of grieve.

Solutions are to be found at the back of the book.

Jane Austen
A Family Life

George and Cassandra Austen produced eight children. James, the eldest, was the most academic, a solemn and conscientious man, equally at home in both the saddle and the pulpit. His daughter, Anna, was close to her Aunt Jane; his son wrote her first biography. Next came the unfortunate George whose disabilities were sufficient to put him into the care of a decent couple. George was never forgotten by his family – financed by siblings after the parents died and Jane was believed to have communicated with him in sign language. Third son, Edward, a loving man who never forgot his family when he was adopted by a rich, distant cousin of his father. He was a capable manager of his estates in Godmersham and Chawton. His eldest daughter, Fanny, was close to her Aunt Jane. Henry came next – oh, what a Henry – a handsome man of charm! More of him later. It must have been a pleasant surprise when the following child was a daughter—Cassandra. Cassandra became engaged to one of her father's pupils but unfortunately, the man died before they were married. Then came another boy, Francis, before a little sister, Jenny, arrived in December 1775. Jenny was Jane, of course. Just one more child, another boy called Charles. Both

Frank and Charles had successful careers in the navy. This loving and clever family all lived and grew up in a rectory situated in a tiny Hampshire village called Steventon.

When Cassandra was to be sent with cousin, Jane Cooper, to Oxford to receive some education from Mrs Cawley, Mrs Austen said that if Cassandra had her head cut off, Jane would want hers cut off too. So, Jane Austen also went to Oxford. After a few months, Mrs Cawley took the girls to Southampton where they caught a putrid fever, nearly died and were taken home by their mothers. The three girls next went to a school in Reading, Berkshire and after a couple of years 'scrabbling an education', returned to Steventon until Mr Austen retired and took his women to Bath. Unfortunately, he died soon afterwards which put the ladies in a fix. For a while, they lived in Southampton before Edward came to the rescue and let them live in one of his cottages in Chawton, Hampshire when, after eight years of successful writing, Jane Austen died in Winchester in July 1817.

Alton	Anna	Basingstoke	Bath	Cassandra
Charles	Chawton	Cooper	Edward	Eliza
Fanny	Frank	George	Godmersham	James
Jane	Oxford	Reading	Steventon	Winchester

1. Mr Darcy's bailiff ran knowing hands down the flanks of the horse before giving his opinion.
2. The handyman went directly to Mr Woodhouse's hencoop, erecting more wire fencing to prevent further attacks by the fox.
3. Mrs Goddard presented the book to her enthralled pupils, who sat in silence as she read in genuine feelings of pathos, anger and joy.

4. Collecting the box for dropping off at the Bates' on the way, Emma put it on the seat beside her and the carriage drove off.

5. The snow on Box Hill provided ample opportunity for the toboggan naturally, but there was insufficient to accommodate anyone on skis.

6. Whatever Edmund said or did for Fanny it was always the best, even to not sparing the effort required.

7. There was essence of yarrow root in her store, but Mrs Morland gave Catherine the syrup of some tonic haw to nip the cough in the bud before it affected her chest.

8. It was a question of whether Maria Lucas, Sandra Phillips or Mary King should take the leading role although neither were really good enough for it.

9. With the application of a little rouge or gentle pinching of the cheeks, her pallor would become less evident when she presented herself to the company.

10. If it hadn't been for the theft, the total to naval funds would have been considerably more worthwhile donating.

Sense and Sensibility

The first Austen book put forward to a publisher was *First Impressions* in 1797. Mr Austen had recognised the talent of his daughter and offered it for publication. But his letter was not much of a sales pitch and the book was returned unread by Thomas Cadell. The next sortie into the publishing world came from Jane herself when she sent a copy of *Susan* to Richard Crosby. But that didn't come to anything either.

Jane Austen seems to have given up any attempt at writing after that besides the beginnings of a novel we know as *The Watsons*. But it was abandoned. However, it appears that over these seemingly barren years, until 1809, when the ladies moved to Chawton, Jane had been revising a couple, perhaps three, books that she had written before the family moved to Bath. One was *Elinor and Marianne* re-named *Sense and Sensibility* and many scholars believe this to have been originally written in an epistolary form which was the common style for novels authored in the eighteenth century.

Having revised this book, converted it into a form that gave more scope to the text and, probably, lifting it into a modern era that we are pleased to call the Regency period—although George IV did not become Regent until 1811 then king in 1820 and died in 1827. But the Regency Period is usually dated from 1795 until 1837 when Queen Victoria ascended the throne.

Austen felt it was ready for submission to a publisher. To do this, she enlisted the help of her brother Henry who was by this time living in London and well established as a banker. Because of his connections with the military, he approached a publisher of military works. Thomas Egerton accepted *Sense and Sensibility* written by A Lady, and published it in 1811.

Allenham	Barton	Brandon	Dashwood	Delaford
Devonshire	Edward	Elinor	Ferrars	Jennings
Lucy	Margaret	Marianne	Middleton	Norland
Palmer	Robert	Steele	William	Willoughy

1. The agitated warden caused a lot of upset and stress amongst the girls of the Young Ladies Seminary in Richmond.
2. Eleanor Tilney dressed in taste, elegant in her white gowns in styles suitable for every occasion.
3. Because of their dreadful grammar, I annexed the whole area until their language was compatible with what was required with the rest of the group.
4. Henry grasped hold of the bar to numb his opponent's arm with a well-aimed hit to the elbow.
5. Edward Knight had become interested in carpentry and particularly enjoyed working on his lathe, so he selected carefully, taking relatively hard ash wood planks from the store in the barn, to make a new leg for the broken chair in the library.

6. It was a difficult manoeuvre as he and his pal merged into the shadows afforded by the rocks, without getting their feet wet.
7. It was a good hotel, in or outside, for the price, and there was no arguing about who went where in the end.
8. She was most upset by the whole affair and neither house nor land would satisfy her, however much money was involved.
9. I think you will, I am sure, want to be involved in the arrangements so that you are satisfied that everything is as you wish.
10. Mr Knightley worked his way through the crowd into the middle, to negotiate with the two boys who didn't look as though they would be able to settle their argument without knocking their heads together.

Pride and Prejudice

With the success of *Sense and Sensibility,* it was time to take *First Impressions* to the publisher. It had been renamed *Pride and Prejudice.* Jane confessed that she had lopped and cropped it, but it needed something more substantial in the text as she felt that it was too light and airy. She called it her 'darling child'. Her copyright was sold to Thomas Egerton who published the book which came out in 1813.

Pride and Prejudice was the first of Jane's novels to be made into a film and the famous (infamous?) production of 1940 starring Green Garson and Laurence Olivier bears only a faint resemblance to Austen's original work. However, the costumes are gorgeous, even if they owe much to the Victorian age.

A landmark production came onto our television screens in 1985 and was dramatised by Fay Weldon who was gaining herself an impressive reputation. Starring Elizabeth Garve and David Rentoul, it was an immediate success. I was most dissatisfied because, like Lizzy, I was completely taken in by Wickham and I had made up my mind that she deserved him. David Rentoul was much too good at being aloof.

The series that had the biggest impact of all on the general public was, of course, Sue Birtwistle's production of 1995 with Jennifer Ehle and Colin Firth in the leading roles. What I particularly liked about it—well, I liked it all actually, but the best bit was that Andrew Davies' adaption kept almost entirely to Austen's script.

Few authors have had as much of their work produced on the small or large screen as has Jane Austen but beware of adaptions as they may confuse what is true to the novel and what is not. A wet shirt and a fencing lesson are cases in point.

Bennet	Bingley	Charlotte	Clapham	Darcy
Gardiner	Hill	Hurst	Jane	Lambton
London	Longbourne	Lydia	Meryton	Netherfield
Pemberley	Rosings	Wickham	William	Young

1. Isabella's eyes sparkled almost as brightly as the lovely diamonds he was about to fasten about her neck.

2. Margaret snatched the ribbon from her sister's hands and offered her thanks with ill grace.

3. Lucy looked at the food on her plate, pushed away the lamb to Nancy and resolved to never eat any red meat ever again.

4. The shawls were piled high—upon shelves already full—on donated and unwanted clothes that might be worth giving to the poor.

5. Charles Bingley adjusted his wife Jane's bonnet, her field of vision thus widened to encompass the complete and unhindered view of their new Staffordshire home that lay before them.

6. The two sisters clung together as the thunderclap hammered their eardrums and the rain-soaked them through to the skin.

7. The boundary took shape as the rounded arc, yet to set thoroughly, gave a pleasant access to the walled garden.

8. It was a great disappointment to the Thorpe family as they walked along Bournemouth high street without finding a single shop that sold hats.

9. Edmund passed the tweezers to Fanny for sterilizing in the pan of hot water before extracting the splinter that was just protruding from Susan's finger.

10. "I assure you that the swill I ambushed you with, will not harm you, but might even improve the texture of your skin," laughed John Thorpe as he looked upon his sister's furious countenance.

Mansfield Park

Mansfield Park is probably the best of Austen's novels for providing material for debate. Is she or is she not writing for the abolition of slavery? Lord Mansfield was instrumental in a landmark lawsuit that decreed there were no slaves in this country and every slave who entered it became a freed slave. There is a very awkward moment in the story when Sir Thomas has returned from his troubled estate in Antigua and Fanny asks him a polite question about his visit. This question is followed by a dead silence.

Does Austen wish to present opposite views about the clergy as illustrated by Mary Crawford and Edmund Bertram? Or was she intending to address the question of Evangelism? She declared in a letter that she was going to write about ordination. There isn't a lot explicitly written in the text about ordination. Dr Gant held the living that was intended to eventually be for Edmund. He was necessary to Austen's plot as his wife's relations—the racy Crawford's—arrived on the scene to disrupt the peace and harmony of the inoffensive Fanny Price. Very little of this in the text appears in detail. A more specific issue arrives at Sotherton where Mary Crawford expresses her disdain for the clergy not knowing Edmund (whom she would quite like to marry) was about to be ordained. Perhaps, it is about ordination. However, despite this faux pas, Edmund continued to fall under her spell. You must read the book if you want to know what happens next. Another subject for debate is that Fanny is like Marmite—you either love her or hate her.

Mansfield Park was accepted for publication in 1813. The novel often drops to the bottom of the list of Austen favourites. The plot is good, but it is the personality of Fanny that irritates some people. Mark Twain wanted to dig Jane Austen up and hit her over the head with her shinbone. I know someone who would like to do that to Fanny Price.

There have been some spin-off versions of the story where authors have swapped the couples who marry. So, who *did* marry whom?

Antigua	Cowper	Crawford	Edmund	Fanny
Francis	Grant	Henry	Julia	Mansfield
Maria	Norris	Price	Pug	Repton
Rushworth	Susan	Thomas	Ward	Yates

1. He was walking around the plantation with his manager and there, before Sir Thomas Bertram's eyes, was a giant iguana, that both frightened and fascinated him.
2. The poor lady ate something that disagreed with her constitution resulting in her death after weeks of suffering.
3. Who cannot but worship ugly ducklings when you know that they will turn into swans?
4. John Thorpe's anger kept him arguing, ranting and generally making himself obnoxious to all and sundry.

5. The leg was too horrific—raw for days after the initial injury and a suppurating mess for weeks afterwards.

6. Religion was supposed to be tolerated in those days tho' Mass had to be observed in secrecy all the same.

7. She deserves more appreciation for accompanying the woman on her travels but barely a French franc is as much as she can expect for reward.

8. Maria was neither wanton nor rising above her station, but at least deserved a little respect for what she tried to be.

9. They discovered that the Geographical Society only needed mundane adjustments and routine inspections from time to time in order for it to function properly.

10. Henry may go on Monday to Moscow perhaps or if not, it will have to wait until Friday because there are no tickets available from Berlin between those two days.

Emma

Jane Austen said that no one would love her heroine but herself. Emma certainly has the potential for being another Lady Catherine de Bourgh. Thank goodness for Mr Knightley. Austen was not correct because many readers quote Emma as their favourite character.

Conditions were different in those days; it was not unusual for families to stay in one village for a lifetime. As a teenager still, her mother dead, her father, the ultimate hypochondriac, cared for by Emma herself (with the help of servants it is true). There were not a lot of opportunities to widen her experiences. After the marriage of her governess, she lacked stimulating conversation. Poor child, no wonder she looked around for amusement. Lots of girls would have rebelled. Emma's fault was in taking her rebellion—looking for relief from a dull day—into the lives of other people.

The novel has more than one cameo character; Mr Elton, the new vicar of Highbury, not quite so crass as Mr Collins (*P & P*) but not so discerning as the vicar of Hunsford when he chose his wife, Augusta. Augusta isn't a deeply bad person like Mrs Norris (*MP*) though. She just isn't very nice. On the other hand, there's dear old, inoffensive, well-meaning Miss Bates. She is the impoverished daughter of a previous vicar of

Highbury and now lives with her widowed mother. The only trouble is her garrulous nature. Bless her. I vote a hug for Miss Bates. Mr Knightley knew her worth.

Some people have called *Emma* a detective story and there are certainly some mysteries in the plot with subtle clues in the text to help you guess the correct outcome.

Another interesting aspect is the use of conundrums in the story. The Austen family were great inventors of conundrums and there is a published volume of their efforts. (See the recommended reading list) when travelling or relaxing during a quiet evening at home. Edward Austen Knight was apparently particularly clever in inventing conundrums.

Augusta	Bates	Churchill	Cole	Donwell
Emma	Fairfax	George	Hartfield	Hawkins
Jane	Kingston	Martin	Randalls	Selina
Suckling	Taylor	Weston	Windsor	Woodhouse

1. To receive such esteem made her feel appreciated if only momentarily.
2. In order to reach Bristol, you must travel west on Mr Brunel's train from London and once you get there you will find plenty of cabs to take you to the church.
3. It was carried on well and truly with his interest at heart so, although it was not quite what he had hoped for, he accepted the offer with good grace.
4. Lizzy didn't care a fig for the king's tonnish friend and snapped her fingers in his face even though it might have resulted in social disgrace.
5. Mary gathered the dandelions, chickweed and groundsel in a basket and took it home for her bantams and rabbits.

6. In the evening there was usually at least one bat, especially flying over the Pemberley stream, catching insects that flew above and around the water.

7. If Mr Gardiner didn't find somewhere to lodge or get someone to put him up, he wouldn't be able to go to his trade meeting in Birmingham.

8. James was proud of his Church art, fielding the negative comments with aplomb and accepting the praise, which he felt was due to him, with a nonchalance that said nothing for his modesty.

9. At the Wedgewood warehouse the storeman was instructed to brand all seconds with a different colour to the china that was perfect.

10. The baby had wind, so Rosalie patted it on the back, hoping to calm the child and get rid of the offending disorder before Mr and Mrs Palmer returned.

Persuasion

Persuasion is the last of Austen's complete novels. It is one of the shortest, perhaps indicating her weakening health. We are lucky to have the original ending which she changed drastically. Perhaps if she was not ailing, she may have developed one of the characters into a more rounded cameo such as Mr Collins, Mrs Norris or Miss Bates. William Walter Elliot could do with a bit of padding out.

It is thought by some people, that Anne Elliot is a portrait of Jane herself. Apparently, in later years, Cassandra Austen let slip to a niece that, whilst they were on holiday on the southwest coast of England, Jane met a young man who wanted to take the friendship further. The tale goes that, although he was keen to meet up again with Jane, he died before this could happen. Was Jane really indulging in wishful thinking by keeping Wentworth alive to be reunited with Anne nearly a decade after they had parted? Rudyard Kipling (*Jane's Marriage*) took Frederick Wentworth to Heaven to marry Jane. Or is there here, an element of the proposal from Harris Bigg Wither? We do know that she accepted his offer of marriage and then changed her mind the next morning. Had Jane persuaded herself that the marriage would solve the Austen ladies' financial problems and the next morning knew that she could not possibly marry without love?

There are some interesting facets to this novel, not least the hint of a changing world. As always Austen never misses an opportunity to include some references to her well-loved poets and authors. Jane also indulges in making her favourite Lyme as a momentary centre of attention and attraction. The novel comes close to home too, as Austen used all her knowledge, gained from her two sailor brothers, to make the navy a prime focus.

After Austen's death, her brother Henry arranged for the posthumous publication of *Persuasion* and *Northanger Abbey* as one unit. As an introduction, he wrote a Notice which could be called the first biography of Austen. Perhaps, he felt that the public should know more about her. Unfortunately, it is rather sugary; a Dear Aunt Jane figure, homely and pious. No one who reads her work or her letters these days could find it a true description of this feisty lady.

Anne	Bath	Benwick	Clay	Croft
Elliot	Frederick	Hayter	James	Kelynch
Louisa	Mary	Monkford	Plymouth	Rooke
Russell	Smith	Wallis	Walter	Wentworth

1. "If you think that wall is too high for me to climb over," said Catherine, "you are very much mistaken, and I will prove you wrong this instant."
2. Henry bowled fast and the bat hardly tipped the ball as Frank sent it soaring over beyond the boundary hedge and into the lane.

3. David was destined to become a monk for devious reasons not acknowledged by his stepfather, but he would not submit to such arrogance without protest.

4. Catherine's preference for the Gothic lay in a desire to be knowledgeable rather than eccentric.

5. Edward took hold of the two-pronged pitchfork to pile the hay, terminating his hard work only when all had been gathered and formed a stack that looked as professional as any farm labourer could build.

6. The servants at Purley Hall were astounded as Mr Warren Hasting's kangaroo kept bounding in front of the house for almost an hour until at last it was cornered by the gardener and stableboy to join the other exotic animals kept there by their owner.

7. The physician Tysoe Saul Hancock told the Ranee, "You can give the Raj a message from me and that is I am confirmed in my original opinion."

8. In 1822, when appointed to the Tower of London menagerie, Alfred Cops brought in 300 more animals as the place had gone into decline and he used the walrus' selling power to attract more visitors.

9. To counteract her toothache, Eliza was told to apply mouth-numbing crushed cloves to the offending area.

10. Because of Lady de Bourgh's authoritarianism, it has destroyed the village spirit and made the community resentful.

Northanger Abbey

Jane Austen loved reading. Her father had so many books that you could almost call it a library and he was eclectic in his taste. From the scholarly classics through poets and playwrights; from Shakespeare to Homer, Locke and Rousseau, Fielding and Johnson, the picturesque (Gilpin), history (Goldsmith), conduct (Fordyce), travel, astrology (Herschel) and military. Jane had access to them all as well as owning her books and borrowing from lending libraries works by Maria Edgeworth, Mary Wollstonecraft, Madam D'Arblay and Hannah Moore. She read the novels of Jane West (*The Gossips Story*) Charlotte Lennox (*The Female Quixote*) Mrs Radcliffe (*The Mysteries of Udolpho*), Samuel Richardson (*Sir Charles Grandison*) and Horace Walpole's *The Castle of Utranto*. Jane relished the Gothic mysteries, laughing at their outrageous plots.

The Austen family were fond of the Arts. It was always a pleasure for Jane to be escorted by her brother Henry to the art galleries in London. The theatre was a favourite too. From her earliest years, Jane was involved in the family theatricals, loving the performance of her glamourous cousin, Eliza de Feuillide and admiring the clever prologues and epilogues penned by her oldest brother, James. Richard Brinsley

Sheridan was a favourite and the burlesque struck a chord with Jane. It shines through in the *Juvenilia* and some spills on into *Northanger Abbey*, where she acknowledges the way an audience or reader could be captivated and frightened.

Northanger Abbey bounces along like a well-written, well-performed play with its ability to make us shiver, to make us laugh at the sardonic and ironic interpretations and sigh at the change in the protagonist, Catherine Morland, who grows in maturity.

Austen could admire and at the same time see faults—for instance, in the picturesque. Whilst maybe ridiculing the overstated nature of her contemporary novels, she still recognises the worth of the author.

Abbey	Allen	Bath	Catherine	Crabbe
Eleanor	Frederick	Fullerton	Henry	Hughes
Isabella	James	John	Morland	Northanger
Richard	Richmond	Thorpe	Tilney	Woodston

1. Once arrived at the ball, engaged for every dance, Lydia was a happier young lady than she had been when she set out in such haste.

2. They are usually to be found in Gawsworth or persuade them to go to Macclesfield if that is what you prefer.

3. Whether you like lean or fatty meat is immaterial to the choice available I'm afraid, so we must make the best of a bad meal.

4. Perhaps if you give Sir Thomas a hug, he surely must respond to such an affectionate gesture or else he is too hard hearted for words.

5. She poured more wine, now fuller to nearer the top of the glass, lest she seemed ungenerous.

6. George was relieved to get out of the woods, to never return there again without a companion.

7. The Making of Bread Act of 1800 prohibited the miller of Meryton from producing flour other than wholemeal, then rye became a consideration as an addition.

8. So, if Maria is always late, is a bell an answer to the problem or can you think of a better strategy?

9. Mr Darcy was rich, ardently in love with Lizzy and therefore should have assured her of a happy future.

10. If crab be your choice with lobster as another preference, then you cannot do better than visit the island and there are regular ferries to Cowes from here.

Sanditon

Only a few chapters of *Sanditon* were written before Austen died. The scrap left to us gives us some indication as to how she rewrote, added deleted the work in progress. As I tap away on my computer, I think how lucky I am. It was like another glorious rebirth of a phoenix when I abandoned my electric typewriter, my Typex, and my carbon copies and bought my Amstrad. Just think how it must have been for someone like Jane Austen to hand-write everything with the meanest of writing implements. She used goose feathers and iron gall ink on small sheets of paper which were expensive and difficult to obtain. I have a friend who can only compose her work by handwriting it—using the convenience of a ballpoint pen on cheap, easily sourced paper—but is always grateful to me as I put it on to my computer and send it to the publisher by attachment. Jane had no spell-check. Would she have persisted with her idiosyncratic misuse of the 'i' before 'e' rule? How many books would she have produced had she some of the benefits of our age?

Austen called it *The Brothers*, but in which direction was *Sanditon* heading? It didn't come to the public's eyes until 1925 and many have authored their idea of its continuation, but none have been so controversial as Andrew Davies' version for television in 2019.

Austen seems to be writing about hypochondriacs with whom she had no patience if her letters are to be believed. But was this about hypochondria or about the growing popularity to develop quiet fishing villages like Brighthelm-stone into a fashionable health spa such as Brighton? The novel could have progressed in any direction.

Ignoring the subject matter in Sanditon, you can detect a change in Austen's approach to the novel. It is almost as if she is developing her genre from Regency to Victorian.

Arthur	Beaufort	Brighton	Brinshore	Brereton
Charlotte	Clara	Denham	Diana	Sanditon
Heywood	Trafalgar	Lamb	London	Mary
Parker	Sidney	Tunbridge	Waterloo	Willingden

1. If, Isabella, you do not wish to be apart, hurry your steps to catch up with your friends.
2. The couple rambled through the neglected garden, hampered by brambles and nettles that caught their clothes and stung their hands.
3. It should not have been difficult for Emma to park, errors in the judgement of the width of the phaeton notwithstanding, as there was plenty of space and few other carriages in the vicinity.
4. Charlotte was keen to invite the beau for tea in order to introduce her sister Maria to a wider circle of eligible men.
5. It was difficult to find willing denizens of the forest to come out of hiding so that we could get to know them better.

6. Although on the short side, Philadelphia found the Hindi an admirable foil for her pale skin and golden tresses.
7. Elinor changed her position as the sun was glaringly bright on that side of the room.
8. The wooden seat was so rough that Frank had to sand it on both sides before applying the paint and clear varnish.
9. She ran away as fast as she could with a bank of overflow water looming threateningly behind her.
10. Mrs Elton's butler speedily went for Lot Six, the gardener bid for Lot Seven but, not so quick off the mark, for the char, Lot Ten was better than nothing.

The Watsons

The Watsons is a bit of a mystery. It is generally accepted as having been written in Bath, in about 1804, a conclusion reached through the paper being watermarked with that date. Why did Austen abandon it? Several reasons have been suggested. One is that the story was taking on a theme too near to home—girls looking for a husband and a father who was about to die. Mr Austen unexpectedly died in 1805. Cassandra and Jane were not looking for husbands, but it would not be surprising if both Mr and Mrs Austen and Mrs Austen's brother, James Leigh-Perrot, and wife who had property in Bath, would be looking on their behalf.

Another suggestion put forward was that Jane had written herself into an impasse and taken the sisters into too lowly an estate. When quizzed later, she had said to whom the heroine, Emma Watson, was to have married.

Some say that Jane was too unhappy to write because she disliked Bath and was despondent through the lack of her success in publication. Those years between 1798 and 1809, when she picked up her pen again, are seen to be barren years. Were they though?

Now living in Bath, Jane had previously known the city when visiting the Coopers there and when her brother Edward took her for a break; she was entertained by her uncle, of whom she was fond and his wife whom she did not like very much. It appears that Jane enjoyed the city then and lapped up its cultural heritage, the years that inspired *Susan* (*Northanger Abbey*). Her last time in Bath was when she lived there and many of us know that when we go to live in a place it does not hold the same charm that it did when we were visitors. Added to this, it was a time of declining income now that Mr Austen had retired and relied on a small amount from his living because he had to pay his son for the curacy. There was little other income and when he died, the Austen ladies were in dire straits.

An unfinished piece of writing is an open invitation to Austen enthusiasts so it should be no surprise to find that many authors have written their version of what happened next. The first was probably in 1850 when Mrs Hubback (Catherine Anne Austen) Jane Austen's niece born after her aunt died, published *The Younger Sister* in three volumes.

Blake	captain	Carr	castle	colonel
Croydon	Edward	Elizabeth	Emma	Howard
Margaret	Musgrave	Osborne	oysters	Penelope
Roberts	Sam	Stanton	Tom	Watson

1. Was it indeed expected of her to marry a man who had a townhouse as well as one in the country?
2. Sergeant Ravenscar reviewed the new recruits with a jaundiced eye and then roared his commands, thus unnerving the squad at the outset.
3. The wretched war damage was not just a physical legacy but one that disabled many a man mentally for the rest of his life.

4. Both arms amputated at Salamanca you say, but still, he manages to earn a living sufficient to support his family?

5. Mrs John Dashwood went wild, constant on one thing only and that was a demand for more money.

6. How, at so nice a place as the Derbyshire Dales, can you possibly not enjoy the walks?

7. It was so clearly an open elopement of Lady Anne Abdy and Lord Charles Bentinck that everyone was able to guess at it and thus no secret at all.

8. Those words must calm us, grave thoughts though they may be, and so we should all pull through in the end

9. The madcap, tainted with a questionable reputation, was no suitable match for their daughter.

10. I must tell you how ardently I admire and love you.

Volume the
First – Juvenilia

Lively youngsters, especially teenagers, love to challenge, shock and mock. If that youngster is intelligent and is tolerated, encouraged even, by her elder siblings and parents, then the result is something like Jane Austen's *Juvenilia*. To some, addiction comes in the form of drink, drugs, smoking, hoarding. Others have a compunction to put pen to paper. In Jane Austen's day people wrote long letters to each other and some whose urge it was to write, acquired satisfaction through that medium. A few, like Jane Austen, wrote stories.

I have said previously that Jane loved burlesque. I have also said that she can enjoy something whilst viewing it with a critical eye. Novels were over the top, in those days, in their storytelling of kidnaps and castles, ravishment and revulsion, of mysteries and mayhem. Many of these stories had settings in foreign lands, giving full rein to the excitement, the exotic, the extreme. Jane lapped it all up, enjoying the sheer outrageous situations, the blood-curdling happenings, the mayhem, mystery and make-believe in which the heroine was placed and the reader hoped for a 'knight in shining armour' to rescue her. And it made Jane laugh.

For the amusement of her family, she wrote her own versions. Shock stories—some only a few sentences long of completely outrageous burlesque. Each one had a dedication. They developed into something different and promising and Mr Austen obviously felt that there was some hidden talent here, that his daughter should be encouraged and the ideas preserved for posterity. 'Write them down, Jane,' and he gave her three exercise books in which she did record them, entitling them Volume the First, the Second and the Third.

The Juvenilia didn't reach the general public until 1925 when published and had a mixed reception. However, as the years have passed, they have become more appreciated and a centre of interest. Perhaps there will be sequels! One of these days I expect we will see them on a screen, 'to laugh at them in our turn'.

Amelia	Alice	aunt	Cassandra	Clifford
Curate	Edgar	Elfrida	footman	Frederic
Harcourt	Green	Jack	Mogul	Stanhope
Sultana	uncle	tripe	partridge	wheelbarrow

1. You cannot rip every piece of paper into shreds that does not satisfy your high expectations.
2. There was the evidence, in just one uneven row, the mark of a shallow heel-bar, rows of footsteps in the muddy ones and plenty of other confusions wherever they searched for the poacher.
3. It was a bedraggled garden that she viewed from the window waiting for him to appear out of the depressing sheets of rain.
4. Given her hesitant good nature, Lizzy was surprised when Jane made herself rid a household of greedy

relations with more grit and gut than she supposed her sister possessed.

5. At Barton Cottage, the Dashwood's had one area of red erica and another of pink but decided that it was sufficient so looked for different hardy plants for the remaining heath-like beds that weren't devoted to vegetables or herbs.

6. Richard thought carefully but, in the end, would agree not to stir an inch more than was necessary.

7. Tom Parker was fun, clever and everything a husband should be apart from his dreadful laugh which sounded like a donkey with constipation.

8. She would never consult a nasty woman like that again however difficult it was to find another expert.

9. Did it never occur, a tender minute, to your unkindness, your unrelenting sarcasm, that the child may have been telling the truth?

10. It was a choice between braving the cliff or descending by the longer route down to the beach.

Love and Freindship
Volume the Second

Jane is now becoming a serious writer but not yet ready to turn this epistolary story into a full-blown novel. *Love and Freindship*, first published in 1922 is a 'novel in a series of letters' – 'Deceived in Freindship and Betrayal in Love'. It is dedicated to 'Madam la Comtesse DE FEUVILLIDE [de Feuillide] this novel is inscribed by her obliged Humble Servant The Author'.

On request, Laura writes to Marianne, her freind's daughter. There is still the presence of burlesque, emerging as exaggeration in the letters:

"My Father was a native of Ireland and an inhabitant of Wales; my mother was the natural Daughter of a Scotch Peer by an Italian Opera girl. I was born in Spain and received Education at a Convent in Wales."

And now, a phrase often quoted by Austen's fans: "Beware, the insipid Vanities and idle Dissipations of the Metropolis of England. Beware of the unmeaning luxuries of Bath and the stinking fish of Southampton."

Letter 5 written by Laura to Marianne is some 400 words in length. It begins with conversation and is all about the 'violent Knocking of the outward Door':

My Father started. "What noise is that?" said he.

"It sounds like a loud rapping at the door," replied my mother.

"It does indeed," I cried.

And so, the conversation goes back and forth, discussing that the continuing knocking at the door must indeed be someone knocking at the door. Eventually, the door is opened to 'the most beautieous and amiable Youth I had ever beheld'. Lindsay is travelling between Bedfordshire and Middlesex via Wales. Laura promptly marries him. After some visiting, travelling, and an arrest, 'This was too cruel, too unexpected, a blow to our gentle sensibility – we could only faint.'

More travelling intricately involved kinships and more fainting. The letters continue in their story of love and freindship, calamity and scoundrels. Adventures, dull theatricals and stagecoach drivers abound.

NB I have kept faithful to Austen's spelling, punctuation and capital letters.

Agatha	Banquo	Cupid	Dorothea	elm
Father	Gilpin	Isabel	Jupiter	Laura
Macbeth	Marianne	Southampton	Sophia	Talbot
Scotland	sister	(St) Claire	Sterling	Wales

1. On that basis, terrible retribution will be brought down upon your head before you know it.
2. Kitty will collect the hats; Lydia will muster lingerie and Maria will bring up the rear with all of the shawls.
3. Observing the exhibits in Mr Jones' emporium of exotic displays, George noted that the basic lair, especially of the big cats, was nothing more impressive than a few shrubs and some rocks.

4. She said that it was below a lesser outcrop of rocks in Lyme Regis where Mary Anning had made her astounding discoveries of fossils.

5. If you do not direct the public up, I do not think they will tolerate seats where they cannot see John Wesley speak.

6. Mary went on and on in a droning voice, quoting liberally from Fordyce's Sermons, her long tale becoming a saga that bored the company to tears.

7. It does not matter from where she comes, she is a beloved friend who will do whatever she can to help.

8. If you total both groups of boys, I will count the number of girls in the other two groups.

9. You can't just ban quotations from Cowper as it will offend the vicar who is very partial to *The Task*.

10. Edmund agreed to counsel more people in a week than he had been undertaking in the past but protested that he would not be able to be so thorough.

Lesley Castle – Also from Volume the Second

To Henry Thomas Austen Esq

SIR, I am now availing myself of the liberty you have frequently honoured me with of dedicating one of my novels to you. That it is unfinished, I greive; yet fear that from me, it will always remain so; that, so far as it carried, it should be so trifling and so unworthy of you, is another concern to Your obliged humble servant.

THE AUTHOR

Messrs Drummond & Co, please to pay Jane Austen, Spinster the sum of one hundred guineas on account of your humble servant.

H T AUSTEN

Note the misspelling of grieve. Austen was also fond of using semicolons.

Miss Margaret Lesley writes to Miss Charlotte Lutterell, addressed from Lesley Castle on January 3, 1792. Jane would have been 17 years old. The tale is amusing for its ridiculousness rather than for burlesque. When a wedding cannot take place because each couple has an accident, the concern of the correspondent was, "What shall we do with the victuals?" The answer, of course, was to eat them and when having made a good start on doing just that, Charlotte Lutterell left the house (taking with her a goodly supply of said victuals) the servants were instructed 'to eat as hard as they possibly could' of what was left behind.

Austen's texts are full of minutiae of complicated relationships, impossible journeys and long lists of, say, food or personal attributes. It is as if Jane is side-tracked by her sense of humour and the need to amuse her family for whom her early works were written. They are almost Shakespearean in their asides. It is interesting to note that although those early works are full of long descriptions of ridiculous bodily features, in Austen's adult novels the very opposite applies.

The situations in *Lesley Castle* are silly there is a confusion of people and random places, and letters often include trivial nonsense. I confess that I found it difficult to follow this story and am not surprised that Jane Austen declared it to be unfinished.

Bristol	castle	Charlotte	concert	doctor
Drummond	Edinburgh	Lesley	London	Lutterell
Margarette	Marlowe	Matilda	Paris	Portman
				(Square)
Shilling	surgeon	Susan	syllabub	veal

1. Their relationship was platonic on certain days but when they were alone it became more intimate.
2. There will be several guests: us and, of course, the Thorpes, plus the Morlands and the Allens making ten in all to sit down to dinner.
3. Stuart will bring the drum Monday, but you may only have its loan for three days, otherwise, it incurs a penalty.
4. I assure you; Mrs Austen will be devilish ill in getting there unless we give her some laudanum or find some better form of transport.
5. It will drag the grammar lower down the scale unless we employ a better tutor for those whose achievement is not up to standard.
6. The cart will have to transport many more loads of stone if the road is to be finished by the end of the month.
7. An idea might be to employ only some of the cast least of all those who cannot remember their words.
8. I will have all of those at the back, please, plus the two in the middle as well as that pretty one at the front of the counter.
9. She was nevertheless a heroic harlot tending the poor and needy when she was both poor and needy herself.
10. The gypsies took the stolen raw rabbit meat from the bag and spread a handful on Donwell Abbey's lawn to entice the dogs away from the stables where they had an eye on a promising colt.

The History of England

Oliver Goldsmith wrote *The History of England from the Earliest Times to the Death of George II* which was abridged in 1774. A volume of this book was in the Austen household and Jane wrote some cryptic comments in the margins. It was this work that she parodied in her composition – *The History of England*

"History is bunk," said Henry Ford. Jane Austen did not go so far as that, but she did present an unorthodox opinion of the past, explaining that the piece was written:

By a partial, prejudiced & ignorant Historian.

She copied it into Volume the Second and her sister Cassandra illustrated it.

One can easily believe that Cassandra's illustrations are cartoons of the family: one of the Henry's, the 5th, may be older brother Henry in his military uniform; Edward, the 6th, the fortunate Edward Austen-Knight; Elizabeth—surely not Mrs Leigh Perrott? Mary Queen of Scots—Jane herself; James—the eldest son: Charles—one little brother. Others could be servants, farmworkers, village residents or other friends or relations. Was Cousin Eliza the model for Lady Jane Grey? Like Lady Jane, Eliza's husband was beheaded.

It is a delightful send-up of history and a good knowledge of facts by the reader makes it all the more enjoyable. Given her age, to Jane's declaration of being partial, prejudiced and ignorant, one could add another adjective: arbitrary.

She confessed that the History was written to vilify Elizabeth and to make a heroine of Mary Queen of Scots.

I love it. The first time I read it (a facsimile with an introduction by Deidre Le Faye), I went right back to the beginning and read it again. It is my favourite of all the early works. What laughs Cassandra and Jane must have had together whilst the History was written by one and illustrated by the other.

Agincourt	Anjou	Armada	Charles	Cromwell
Drake	Edward	Elizabeth	Essex	Fotheringay
Henry	Percy	Perkin	Pomfret	Protector
Pym	Spain	Stuart	York	Woodville

1. It is true that whether she is neither happy or kind, you will always be drawn to a person who smiles like that.
2. As they looked at the book together, Margaret Dashwood was assured by Edward that it was indeed a great man jousting on the beautifully caparisoned horse with plaited mane and flowing tail.
3. Jane found it difficult to pamper kinship when she disliked her Aunt Austen-Leigh so much.
4. Cassandra and Jane were gathered together at the spa in the centre of Cheltenham for their health, but it was also a good opportunity to socialise.

5. Miss Carteret was bedecked in jewellery including a circlet upon her head, and on her arm, a dazzling array of bracelets, not to mention the rings on nearly every finger.

6. To ensure that her family understood why she would marry Lieutenant Price, Frances Ward decided that less explanation would be a better strategy.

7. Nothing will ever hamper cynicism when such a worldly-wise person gives vent to her feelings.

8. Charlotte Collins was such a happy mother as she watched her children collecting daisies to make into a chain.

9. The costume was not to her liking, so Harriet fiddled with the pompom, fretting all the while and wishing that she had chosen to be something other than Harlequin's Columbina.

10. Kitty stared at the gentleman and wondered if some show-off other—in gay abandon—would make a fool of himself in such company.

Lady Susan

Correspondence written in this epistolary short novel is written by more characters than in Austen's other similar early work. These letters are different in that the story is a rounded one and there is little of the obvious attempt at burlesque. It is a grownup story—one known as her *Minor Works*—and reflects Austen's observation of human nature and peculiarities. It is moving towards the full-length novels.

Lady Susan Vernon is described as the 'most accomplished coquette in England; a distinguished flirt; has celebrated attractive powers and other such like'. She splits two marriages, takes a lover away from a young lady with the intention of marrying her daughter, Frederica, to him and at the same time considers marrying him herself: she is a widow of four months looking for a rich husband. Lady Susan also endeavours to entrap Reginald de Courcy with whom Frederica is in love. In true Jane style, all of these people are related, mostly by marriage.

The relationship between Lady Susan and her daughter is not good. The woman bullies the girl and sends her off to school from where Frederica runs away. There is a hint of Shakespearean comedy in the tale.

Does lady Susan get her man and if so whom? Does Frederica escape her mother's persecution and does she win the heart of de Courcy? Was Lady Susan the victim of malicious gossip as she claims or was she indeed the scheming, bewitching coquette declared by those who crossed her path?

Lady Susan was made into a film in 2016, directed by Whit Stillman and given the title of another piece of Austen's work—*Love and Freindship*.

Alicia	Cath(erine)	Charles	Churchills	Clarkes
Daughter	de Courcy	Frederica	Johnson	Langford
Lover	Manwaring	Martin	mother	Parklands
Reginald	Smith	Summers	Vernon	Wigmore(St)

1. They were very thankful that the cat had her kittens in the barn rather than in the kitchen.
2. It was a dreadfully inhuman war in gigantic proportions though the dictator denied it.
3. If you think of humanism, it has a certain ring of hopefulness.
4. Although it was touch and go, Henry did, with the aid of the Regent's surgeon and Jane's dedicated nursing, recover nonetheless, for which mercy everyone was relieved.
5. The maid was deceitful over and over again and, in the end, they had to turn her out of the house without a reference.
6. Cubism art in the early twentieth century was a revolutionary approach to representing reality.

7. Naming them Teepee and Pigwig more or less spoke volumes for the inventive imagination with which the child named her toys.

8. Lydia thought it a fantastic lark, especially as it did no one any harm and provided her with a great deal of fun and laughter.

9. On top of Mount Ararat, a damp ark lands and Noah with his sons—Ham, Seth and Japheth—looks out and espies the rainbow.

10. The flowers were mostly sent from admirers and a few came from other friends in Meryton.

Plan of a Novel

In 1816, Jane Austen had a bit of fun by returning to her earlier habit of parodying what was ridiculous in the popular literature of earlier days. When *Emma* was about to be published and the Prince Regent—a fan—heard that she was in London, he arranged for his librarian, James Stanier Clarke, to give her a tour of the library at Carlton House. Subsequently, Clarke wrote to Jane Austen suggesting a plot for her next novel. It was partly this encounter (which resulted in *Emma* being dedicated to the Prince) and perhaps 'helpful' advice from family and friends added to Stanier Clarke's effusive suggestions, that Jane drew up this *Plan of a Novel*.

In one of her letters, Jane had written 'pictures of perfection make me sick and wicked'. She was not impressed by villainous ravishers, high-toned literary sentiments and impassioned emotions preferring a natural depiction of real life. But here, in this *Plan*, she bows to it all. She made marginal notes in her *Plan* with names of friends and correspondents responsible for the 'hints'. These marginal notes were omitted from the version first printed in James Edward Austen-Leigh's *Memoir of Jane Austen* (1870). Some of these helpful people whose names were omitted by JEAL in his *Memoir* have been included in the list of words.

The manuscript of *Plan of a Novel* descended from Cassandra Austen to the family of the younger brother, Charles Austen, and it was made available to Austen-Leigh by Charles' daughter when preparing the *Memoir*. Eventually, descendants of this family offered for sale in 1925 a small collection of Jane Austen's manuscripts. *Plan of a Novel, according to hints from various quarters* was acquired by the Morgan Library, New York. R W Chapman was involved and soon published this piece of tongue-in-cheek writing of Austen's in the 1920s.

Chaplain	Clarke	Cooke	Court	Craven
Critic	depraved	Fanny	Gifford	heroine
Infamous	Knight	marriage	naval	sentiment
Speech	starved	style	tithes	wicked

1. Whenever she was present, I mentioned his name, knowing very well that it annoyed her immensely.
2. The Parson travelled as far north as to Berwick, educating the poor and unfortunate in every village where he stopped.
3. Marianne was too hasty leaving the company in distress so nobody knew where she was going or how long she would be or whether she would return at all.
4. It was a sticking point and Anna valiantly kept to her own opinion even though her stepmother was most unhappy about the whole situation.
5. It was a comic rave Neddy acted out in the Austen theatricals performed in their barn that winter.
6. Yesterday it was the Iambic our tourist guide took us to and we found these columns much more to our liking striking a balance between the Corinthian

which were too fanciful or the Doric which were too plain.

7. Lizzy was practising her French but when it came out as the *'Roi ne pas'* she thought perhaps that she hadn't got it quite right when Georgiana gave a little giggle.

8. It was a risky business to up the anti the same way that he had done in the past.

9. Some thought that it was nevertheless wrong if, for different reasons, Wickham went about charming the newest heiress to arrive in the town.

10. To be frank, nigh ten times as many sheep would not compensate for the loss Sir Thomas sustained in the snowstorm.

Letters I

The first book of published letters was a collection gathered together by Edward, Lord Brabourne (which were arbitrary and sometimes incorrect), an Austen descendant. A landmark edition was published by Oxford in 1932 with the 2nd edition in 1952 edited by R W Chapman. But the most comprehensive book of Jane Austen's letters was compiled by Deidre Le Faye, also published by the Oxford University Press, in 1995. Her edition includes an informative introduction and useful biographical and topographical indexes.

Not all of the letters are from Jane to her sister, Cassandra, but most are. Although Jane must have written thousands of letters to her sister, only 161 have so far come to light (at the time of writing). Unfortunately, Cassandra destroyed most of the letters before passing on the surviving ones, or parts of some, to the family. It is believed that she destroyed the letters to protect both Jane and some members of the family. Perhaps, also, she saw a future when such letters would be interesting for public viewing and Jane's family were very protective of their privacy. It is possible that the images of 'Dear Aunt Jane' might be shattered if her letters were made public. There is always the hope that more will turn up.

The letters reside in several places: The Jane Austen House Museum in Chawton, of course; in the British Library, libraries and museums in both this country and the United States of America; in private hands including descendants of the Austen family. Now and again, a letter or fragment comes up for sale (there was one in October 2020) but not one that had not been tracked down by Deidre. Sadly, Deidre Le Faye died in August 2020 and although there are many scholarly Austen authorities still commenting upon and making discoveries about her life, one wonders who will wear the mantle of the next edition of the *Letters*.

Account	Basingstoke	Bath	Charmouth	date
Dear	friend	Henrietta(St)	ink	irony
Lyme	paper	Pen	post	signature
Sister	Sloane (Sq)	Southampton	travel	weather

1. It was Wickham's loan even though he denied ever knowing anything about it.
2. There was no hope, not in a month of Sundays, of ever having the debt repaid.
3. There was no sign at urethra exits, nor in the whole of the canal, that the disease was being harboured by Mr Knightley's cows and he was relieved that he would not have to have them destroyed.
4. Edward Knight had worried that there appeared to be widespread and prolific harm out Hampshire way although it seemed to be under control now.
5. Colonel Brandon did not want any reward in cash, but if the Dashwoods wished they might send him something in kind.

6. Elinor was only measuring the distance from the door to the window so that she knew how large a carpet the room could accommodate.

7. The meetings were non-stop, ostensibly to cater for those students who came newly to the university and needed something to give them confidence.

8. He was stymied at every turning and became so frustrated that he let out an almighty scream as he pounded the door with his clenched fist.

9. My own beloved earth, how I extol thee and how I bless thee for producing such wonderful potatoes.

10. Miss Bates is terribly upset you know and there is nothing that we can do to make it any better for her.

Letters II

The first published letters date from 1798 and the last, dated July 1817, is from Cassandra to Fanny Knight commenting on the death of Jane Austen. There are some business letters included regarding the publishing of her novels and one or two to relatives but by far the most are the ones to Jane's sister Cassandra. For most of their lives, the sisters were together of course, but occasionally, one or the other would be visiting or staying with a relative or friend so that is when the letters were written. Thus, there are many gaps for this reason.

Some people have complained that there is nothing but domestic news in the letters and none about the events of the day—the Napoleonic Wars, politics, food riots, machine breaking or other remarkable events. However, although not specifically referred to, there are certainly hints that Jane was well aware of what was going on in the world beyond her existence. Her two youngest brothers were involved in the French wars at sea and her cousin's husband was guillotined. Warren Hastings had close connections with Jane's cousin, Eliza (whom Henry Austen married), and also with both George Austen and his wife, Cassandra Leigh. Thus, the family were very much interested in his impeachment. There were remote connections with the slave trade although the

Austens were very much against it. The Leigh wealth came mostly from the silk trade. Jane possibly had mentioned events and politics in the letters that were destroyed.

What we do learn is Jane's brush with romance with Tom Lefroy, of her holidays, of the close relationships she had with her nephews and nieces. We know about her shopping habits, a little bit about fashion and travel, that she enjoyed the theatre and going to art exhibitions; we discover the books and poetry that she read. We know where she stayed and with whom she stayed.

Now and again, we learn whom she likes and who she doesn't. We find that she sometimes had a sarcastic or withering tongue which she presumably only shared in the privacy of her letters to Cassandra. Some of her comments are downright unkind. But she can be ironically funny, touchingly tender and honestly helpful and generous.

Blackall	Bookham	Canterbury	Dartford	Deptford
Digweed	Dummer	Ibthorpe	Itchen	Keane
Kintbury	Knatchbull	Ogle	Overton	Papillon
Plumptre	Rowlings	Sackree	Sherborne	Wyards

1. "You can take an economy seat on the stage, Miss Morland, and be home without any trouble at all," said General Tilney, with withering effect.

2. Isabella grabbed the cameo, gleefully running away from James and hiding behind a shrub to study his silhouette before he could snatch it back from her.

3. Young ladies such as Miss Lydia B lack all the accomplishments necessary for an eligible marriage.

4. In the shop window, yards upon yards of muslin, tulle and other delectable material hung in beautiful, beguiling rainbows of promise.

5. The Dashwoods decided to grow ling simply because it would be the only plant capable of surviving in that bleak spot in their garden.

6. The plump, trembling hand of The Dowager Lady Dalrymple grasped her binoculars, holding them up to peruse the company and thus dismissing her upstart Elliot relations.

7. Looking at the two green sprigs in her hand, Elinor wondered if she should add the woman's herb or nettle to the brew to make it more palatable.

8. With cunning Willoughby took her to the window where he showed an appreciation of landscaped art (for devious reasons known only to himself) and, combined with charm, he completely deceived the innocent girl with whom he had questionable designs.

9. Mrs Bennet and her two youngest daughters were driven over to Netherfield, ostensibly to be assured of the welfare of Jane but they all had their own hidden agenda.

10. Emma blissfully assumed that she was adequately adept for drawing the likeness of Harriet to please Mr Elton.

Textual Strategies

A study of the text in Jane Austen's novels will reveal the emergence of the repetition of certain words. If these words are not used, then the meaning of such are written in another, more effective way.

Two very similar words—*aimable* and *amiable*—had common usage in Regency England and can be found prolifically in contemporary novels. Warren Roberts (*Jane Austen and the French Revolution*) explains, 'to be amiable was to be genuinely but quietly concerned for others, as from a distance; to be aimable was to give an impression of concern and to be superficial and false. To be mannered in one sense was to be forthright in the other indirect and mysterious. One pattern of conduct was English, the other French.' Mr Knightley suggested to Emma that Mr Churchill's behaviour owed much to the French interpretation.

'*Truth*' is also used liberally in Austen's texts: half-truth, untruths, concealing the truth, simple truth, truth revealed, painful truth and the antonym falsehood. '*Silence*' is used as a strategy or for effect rather than as a straight-forward noun: when Elizabeth broke the silence as she danced with Darcy (*P & P*); the silence after Emma's unkind words on Box Hill (*E*); Mrs Norris could only 'hold her tongue' (*MP*). The Tilney's and Catherine fell into silence after the subject of politics was reached (*NA*); Wentworth was 'in an agony of silence' when Maria fell from the Cobb (*P*). then there was the 'dead silence' already referred to when Fanny queried Sir Thomas about Antigua (*MP*).

In the same way, the adjective 'to blush' is used straightforwardly and expressed in a roundabout way. A blush, of course, does not necessarily reveal a person's true feelings. Catherine Morland was 'unable to read' Isabella's blush (*NA*). Fanny's 'face was scarlet' when rejecting Henry Crawford. She had a 'glow of indignation' when the subject was brother William (*MP*).

Following are twenty words found commonly and extensively in the novels. They are of the time.

admirable	agreeable	amiable	aimable	artifice
benefactor	blush	deserve	elegant	esteem
fortitude	fortune	genteel	manner	modest
mortify	reason	silent	taste	truth

1. Oh, *mon ami*, a bleeding heart is a sorrowful state but tomorrow the sun will surely shine for you.
2. "I am most disappointed," said Mrs Norris. "I lent the book to you, Fanny, thinking it would improve your secretive ways."
3. With the threat of doom, Ann erred on the side of caution to prevent any such thing happening.
4. Darcy was furious with the servant as tempers were not tolerated at Pemberley.
5. Of a good crop of ripe strawberries, Mr Knightley was sure, as on every day for the past month the sun had shone warmly and the rain had fallen lightly.

6. John Thorpe was stuck in the first rut, his hands on the reins pulling quite in the wrong direction with too much force and the horses were almost out of control.

7. Whatever the cook made, served on a suitable platter, it was always appreciated by the company.

8. Eleanor, dressed in white, a la mode, stood in the doorway in all her elegance, causing a pause in the conversation.

9. "Well, Bella, I'm able to find plenty of excuses to oblige Miss Morland, but I'm d - - - - d if I'll do the same for you, my dear sister."

10. Mrs Hill thought that the cake would look smart if iced delicately with a pink rose and green marchpane leaves to set it off.

Publication

In 1803, Jane Austen was paid £10 by Crosby & Co for the proposed publication of *Susan*. But it did not see the light of day. A few years later, Austen wrote to Crosby, suggesting that it might be lost and offered to furnish him with another copy. Crosby's answer was brief and hostile. He had the right to publish it when he thought fit and would act against anyone else who did so—or she could buy it back for the price he paid for it. £10 was more than Jane could afford. In 1816, however, on her instructions, brother Henry bought it back. The heroine's name was changed from Susan to Catherine and the book was published with the new title of *Northanger Abbey*. Thomas Egerton was the first publisher of Austen's books and then John Murray. *The Watsons* was abandoned and *Sanditon* began when Jane died. Henry went on to see *Northanger Abbey* and *Persuasion* published in a combined edition

For the next forty-odd years, Austen's novels almost fell into obscurity although there were reminders when Bentley produced his Standard Novels between 1833 and 1869. The biography/memoir published by her nephew in 1870 renewed interest, but when Dent produced a series with an editorial comment in 1892, it lifted Austen's reputation. The Peacock edition (so named because of its cover) of *Pride and Prejudice* which came out in 1894—one of a series published by George Allen and illustrated by Hugh Thomson—gave her books the impetus that would once more bring her to the fore of notable authors in the eye of the general public. Brock (1900s) was another illustrator of note.

By the 1920s – 30s, more of Austen's writing had come to light, notably her *Juvenilia*. Known as the Chapman editions for his scholarly research and introductions, a set was published by the Oxford University Press. He continued to publish and comment on Austen's work until 1954. Since then, most well-known publishers have brought out notable sets of the novels and there have also been some cheap editions too. The novels are now published worldwide in many different languages. The lasts significant complete set is the Cambridge Edition numbering nine books as they include the *Juvenilia, Minor Works* and *Austen in Context*.

author	Brock	Chapman	child	critique
Crosby	darling	editor	Egerton	Henry
ivory	memoir	Murray	novel	Peacock
pewter	Regent	standard	Stanier(Clarke)	Thomson

1. If eating brown bread is not working then rye is maybe the answer or perhaps a loaf that is seeded might help.
2. There was the evocative perfume of cedar lingering in her bedroom that took me back to my childhood and the soap that Nanny used in my bath.
3. You are, gentlemen, the very epitome of what is best about England and I am proud to call you my friends.
4. I did beg 'er to not go oop that thar path yer H'onner but she would do so and with that thar 'eavy bag a

'draggin' of be'ind 'er, she was sure ter come ter grief, yer H'onner, Sir Thomas, sir.

5. The Gardiners' daughter had either combed it or done something different to the doll's hair making it look newer than it actually was.

6. George Austen and James, his son, inspected every pew, termites having infested some of the rafters and they worried that the creatures might find their way into all of the woodwork in the church.

7. The stream was just a murmur, rays of a gentle sun blessing the ripples with a sparkling light that completed the idyllic scene enjoyed by Marianne and Willoughby.

8. Frank gritted his teeth as he made the climb, rocking the branches as he went from one to another in an effort to rescue the stranded cat.

9. Don't fret, Tristan. I erased that mistake long before anyone could take offence.

10. Elinor searched the rolls of cloth, but she could find no velvet the colour to match or compliment the gown that Marianne would be wearing for the coming ball.

Pewter

In 1814, Jane Austen wrote to her niece, Fanny Knight: "People are more ready to borrow and praise than to buy—which I cannot wonder at—but though I like praise as well as anybody, I like what Edward calls pewter too." To her brother, Frank, in 1813, she had written, "I have now therefore written myself into £250—which only makes me long for more." Austen did not make a fortune in publishing but at least, was able to contribute at last to household expenses and have a little over to spend on other things besides necessities.

Fortune was important when considering marriage and Austen often quotes the worth of prospective bride or groom: the £5,000 of Bingley, £10,000 of Darcy, £10,000 of Miss King (*P & P*) for instance. Willoughby married for money (*S & S*), Frederick Wentworth makes his fortune at sea which makes him more eligible (*P*) and General Tilney is hoodwinked over Catherine Morland's prospects (*NA*).

In real life, money played an important part in the Austen fortunes. There was excitement in the family when Mrs Austen's brother was a possible heir to the Leigh title and fortune. When Mr Austen died, the women would have become destitute if it hadn't been for the support from the boys. Henry was a successful banker until, like many others, the bank crashed after Waterloo. Edward, who had inherited Godmersham and a fortune lost a sizeable investment when Henry's bank collapsed and in fees when his Knight inheritance was challenged.

There was disappointment in the family when Mrs Austen's brother left his fortune to his wife. When the expectation of a share in this fortune did not materialise, it was contributory towards Jane's failing health.

annuities	bank	bankrupt	business	capital
coin	economic	entrepreneur	earn	finance
fortune	income	inherit	investment	pewter
profit	prospects	speculate	thousand	wages

1. Once again, her itinerary included Chawton, Alton, Andover and Winchester.
2. Whatever the charade, James was able to cap it always with a better one of his own.
3. Fakes were easily detected in his Cubism works but in his Art Deco no microscopic inspection ever exposed his forgeries.
4. It may work with a G-clef or tune it to a better in C.
5. Hear no evil, see no evil, speak no evil.
6. The stagecoach took Henry to a cold and blustery Oban, keeping him from alighting and thus he continued his journey into the heart of Scotland without even stepping into an inn for a mulled wine.
7. Jane could not understand how age should determine whether or not she was ready to be sent away to school.
8. Lack of fortune would not curb us in essentials but there would be no money for the elegancies of life.

9. James Austen's horse was clumsy in negotiating the steep bank, rupturing its spleen, breaking a foreleg and thus ending all hope for a promising mount for the Vine Hunt.

10. Mr Woodhouse would be laid in his coffin come the winter and the Knightley's would establish themselves in Donwell before the spring.

Literature

In the eighteenth century, a bluestocking was an intellectual, thinking woman. Besides many who acquired accomplishments that would raise them in the eyes of society, there were also a few who were well-informed in the sciences (Caroline Herschel, for example, sister of astronomer William). Early in the 18th century published writers were poets, commentators, politicians et al—all men. As the century progressed, however, more women became writers although not a 'respectable' occupation. Novels by both men and women were read openly by such people as Isabella Thorpe (*NA*) Lydia and Kitty Bennet (*P & P*), Lucy and Nancy Steele (*S & S*) and the Musgrove sisters (*P*). Ladies in real life read the romances too, but unlike Jane Austen, did not always admit to it.

Jane Austen read the books of many authors who were members of the Bluestocking Society (e.g., Fanny Burney) as well as Edgeworth and Wollstonecraft. Jane was interested in women's rights, especially in education. A tale is told that she was once invited to a dinner where she would be a fellow guest of Hester Piozzi (Mrs Thrale). Austen had a withdrawing nature and had no wish to attend this dinner and become a 'celebrity'. Virginia Woolf certainly thought that had she lived longer, Austen would have become a celebrity amongst writers.

During Austen's lifetime, there were two ways for a woman to become educated (as opposed to acquiring accomplishments from a governess or attending a girls' school). One was to grow up in a household where the father (an intellectual man himself) believed that his daughters had a right to knowledge. The other opportunity was through reading. Jane Austen was fortunate in both respects.

We know some of the books that Jane Austen read from her letters and from the authors whom she mentions in her novels. They are wide-ranging and some surprising. She read Charlotte Lennox's *The Female Quixote* more than once and a favourite, *Sir Charles Grandison*. But she also read *Travels in Spain* and *An Essay in Institutions in the British Empire*. Her uncle, James Leigh Perrot, gave her a wide selection of non-fiction books from his collection. Some favourite poets were Shakespeare, Cowper and Pope.

Anhalt	Burns	Byron	Clarissa	Campbell
Cowper	Edgeworth	(Dr)Johnson	Grandison	Inchbald
Radcliffe	Otranto	Pope	Richardson	Scott
Shakespeare	Thompson	Udolpho	Voltaire	Wildenheim

1. It was not an easy task, but Harriet shooed off Mr Martins cow, permitting the child to pass through the gate without too much of a problem.
2. Without thought, he threw off his nightgown and pulled the long johns on before reaching for his trousers and shirt.

3. "Don't worry, Marianne, "said Colonel Brandon, "the grand is on its way and will be in the salon in time for tuning before our guests arrive."

4. The children went chasing round the room, screaming as the soap bubbles gave a delightful pop every time one burst and showered them with droplets of soapy water.

5. The cat entered the room with sleek negligence then jumped up onto the baby's cot to sleep in peace for the rest of the afternoon.

6. Harry was spoiled dreadfully and, with a little trot, ran to Mrs Palmer to complain about the lack of attention he was receiving.

7. "You should put a clean halter on the horse, Maria if you are to impress Mr Rushworth," said Tom.

8. In the temple, they came across a tub-urn such as was found in the ancient society who had lived in the valley below.

9. Whilst they stayed at the camp, bells rang out to call them to a meal but on the march, it was the drums that kept them in order.

10. Mary was charmed by rondos and wondered if her tutor could introduce her to Mozart's Turkish Rondo which was a very fast one.

Landmark Advances

Jane's fame grew gradually at first and then in an almighty rush during the twentieth century, culminating today in a worldwide fan club.

It is not just her novels that have filled the bookshelves. The Edwardian era saw the beginning of scholastic non-fiction when academics realised that Austen's writing was something rather out of the ordinarily clever. Others began to see hidden meanings, saw a different personality emerging from her writing.

Neither was it only commentators who were taken with this author. Other fans emerged and well-known men and women confessed their admiration of Jane Austen. The term 'Janeite' was originally coined by the literary scholar George Saintsbury in 1894 and Rudyard Kipling used this term to effect in his book *Debits and Credits*. Harding (*Regulated Hatred*) accused some who disseminated Austeniana.

The descendants of George and Cassandra Austen began to release more of Jane's writing—the *Juvenilia,* for example, her letters and more about the lives of herself and her siblings. Lord Brabourne was the first to publish a volume of letters and *Jane Austen's Sailor Brothers* was published by the Hubback's.

One of the most scholarly works came out in the first half of the twentieth century when the Oxford University Press produced *The Works of Jane Austen* 'collected and edited from first editions and manuscripts by R W Chapman'. It began an avalanche of many collections by the most reputable of publishers—and cheap editions too—as well as the hundreds of scholarly works looking at every aspect of what can be found in the texts. More was discovered about her life and biographies emerged. Elizabeth Jenkins wrote the first of many good ones. Jenkins was a founding member of The Jane Austen Society in 1940.

Continuations of unfinished works, prequels, sequels and spinoffs appeared. Theatre, the big and small screens, all played their part in familiarising the general public with Austen's novels and her life.

Reputations have been made and continue to be made by scholars responsible for landmark discoveries and insights into the work and life of Jane Austen.

Austen-Leigh	Brabourne	Brock	Butler	Cecil
Chapman	Clery	Doody	Duckworth	Hubback
Jenkins	Lane	Lascelles	Le Faye	Mitton
Southam	Todd	Tomalin	Trilling	Wiltshire

1. As Charles Bingley looked down at his baby son, dangling his fob, rocking the cradle and crooning a lullaby, he was the proudest father in the whole of Staffordshire.

2. He runs, he shouts out, "Hampson, come back, all is well." But the man does not listen and is soon out of sight.

3. Catherine tended to call an eagle a bird of prey but, after Henry's gentle encouragement, in future she called it a raptor—rather like his father, she thought.

4. Darcy walked Lizzy by the Pemberley stream and crossed where it divided into a sweet rill in green pastures and where it gave a romantic touch to the whole scene.

5. It was a strenuous climb up but at midday they had reached the summit, to Nancy's relief, and they would almost certainly be back at the lodge in time for tea.

6. Anne thought that she saw a phantom, a lingering likeness of the man she still loved.

7. The coffee house was a central hub, back in the eighteenth century, for meetings of men with like minds.

8. Lizzy thought it odd that a young lady such as her friend Charlotte Lucas should consider marrying the buffoon, Mr Collins.

9. It was not possible to undo Odysseus' rather scruffy likeness from Emma's efforts at embroidering slippers for Mr Knightley but perhaps he would not notice.

10. It was just a little tipple Fay enjoyed that evening before retiring to bed, but she resolved that she would not imbibe again.

Controversy

Surprise! Surprise! Not everyone liked the novels of Jane Austen. We have already noted some adverse remarks made by Mark Twain and Charlotte Bronte. Why did such prominent artists dislike the books? They could surely not contest the ability of the lady to write a competent, grammatically correct, well-constructed piece of work. No, it was the content or perhaps lack of what they thought should be contained. Novels of Austen's time were expected to be dramatic, adventurous and passionate or even evangelical like Hanna Moore's *Caleb in Search of a Wife*. Yet here were novels about ordinary people doing ordinary things. The cleverness of Austen was the observances of how ridiculous, mistaken, nasty, even boring, ordinary people can be, "I got the book and studied it. And what did I find? An accurate daguerreotyped portrait of a commonplace face…I should hardly like to live with her ladies and gentlemen in their elegant but confined houses," wrote Charlotte Bronte. And Ralph Waldo Emerson said, that "All that interests any character introduced in Austen's novels is still this one: Has he or she the money to marry with, and conditions conforming?…Suicide is more respectable." He was 'at a loss to understand why people hold Miss Austen's novels at so high a rate'.

Kingsley Amis loathed Fanny Price. Cardinal Newman declared that: "Miss Austen has no romance. What vile creatures her parsons are!" There is no end of Mark Twain's anti-Austen comments quoted here, there and everywhere. Here is another: "Just the omission of Jane Austen's books alone would make a fairly good library out of a library that hadn't a book in it." D H Lawrence called her 'this old maid'.

Some comments are just plain controversial: "Stupid people sometimes complain that there is no sex in Austen's novels…Actual sexual intercourse is the off-stage climax of the Austen novel (Germaine Greer)." Although a fan, Emma Thompson thought that Elinor Dashwood was 'just the sort of person you'd want to get drunk, just to make her giggling and silly'.

Some people change their minds. Mary Russell Mitford, having described Jane unbecomingly, in the end, praised her books.

Adverse	Amis	boring	Bronte	comment
Common	confined	content	critic	Emerson
Garson	loathed	Mitford	Newman	omission
Ordinary	(Fanny) Price	romance	Thompson	Twain

1. Catherine escaped to a secret arbor in great haste to avoid meeting with the rather amorous soldier.
2. He sat on the summit for days, his food supplies dwindling at an alarming rate until he was eventually rescued.

3. The housekeeper was making sandwiches for the picnic and kept in mind that ham is Emma's favourite filling.

4. In that particular sitcom, men tended to be the better at delivering the jokes.

5. He was a landlord in Aryan appearance and in Aryan behaviour and was the most popular Aryan host in the town.

6. On the Brecon, tents tended to be buffeted alarmingly and could be blown away if not securely pegged.

7. With aplomb, Ron tended the girl's ankle, believing it to be a pretence to gain his attention.

8. Mr Collins took too much sugar so no wonder his teeth were deteriorating at an alarming rate.

9. When James arrived, he called in for a quick 'Hello' at Henry's stables before walking up the hill to find the man himself.

10. Edmund's attempt at reading Cowper turned out to be badly read verse even in Elinor's opinion.

The Church

As a daughter of the Reverend George Austen, with two brothers, ordained as well as numerous cousins, uncles and friends also men of the cloth, it is no wonder that such people should feature in Jane Austen's novels.

Sense and Sensibility, the first published success, features a heroine whose love interest becomes a clergyman. On the other hand, certain types of clergies are ridiculed. In *Pride and Prejudice*, Mr Collins is a crass cameo character that has 'delighted us all'. Another hero in the third novel, *Mansfield Park*, becomes ordained during the tale. Once more, the clergy are not seen in the best light when Mr Elton appears as a caricature in *Emma*. Henry Tilney charms us in *Northanger Abbey*—he is the best of them all; well, as a man anyway. I must confess to a partiality. Even the unfinished story of *The Watsons* has a father in holy orders and another is a possible husband.

Not so in *Persuasion* or *Sanditon*. That is, neither stories have a major figure in holy orders although *Persuasion* gives a nod to the church in the Hayter family and Dr Shirley. Had the novel continued, maybe Jane would have introduced a man of the Church into *Sanditon*.

A big issue of the day was Evangelism and Jane Austen was not sure that she liked this new attitude to religion. We have a hint when she writes, "We do not much like Mr Cooper's [cousin] new sermons." But later refers more generously to the 'Evangelicals' when planning to read *Coelebs in Search of a Wife* (Hannah Moore). After brother Henry took Holy Orders in 1816, however, Jane wrote of 'Henry's excellent sermons'.

Another issue was 'pluralism' when a pastor had responsibility for more than one Church and paid a curate to take on some of the duties. Jane appears to accept this state of affairs as a norm, perhaps a necessity. It was a time of religious ferment and many changes. Did it please or worry her? Perhaps the absence of religion in *Persuasion* and *Sanditon* indicates that those new ideas with which she needed to grapple were the reason that she felt unable to write about the subject with any certainty.

aisle	Church	clergy	Collins	congregation
curate	Elton	Evangelical	Grant	Hayter
incumbent	living	Methodist	parsonage	pastor
pluralism	rector	Reverend	sermon	tithe

1. If Catherine did not stand erect or at least give him her complete attention, General Tilney was dismissive of her questions.
2. Captain Frederick Wentworth looked up as torrid waters fell fast and furiously down the inside of the ship and into the bilge below.
3. The Reverend Samuel Cooke looked on, astounded that such urchins should be so ungrateful at his generous gesture.

4. Catherine applied herself to the embroidery as the never ever ending of the task threatened to spoil an afternoon of cricket with her brothers.

5. Maurice was the biggest loser Monty had ever met.

6. The whole strategy will gel tonight and thus our future ensured.

7. It was an almost dead bluetit Henry rescued from the jaws of the cat and he hoped that Jane would work her magic on the pathetic bird.

8. Singing did not occur at every service, but it was always a pleasure when it did.

9. The farm labourers tossed the hay, terrifying any animal that may have been trapped there, much to the enjoyment of the men and sport for the dogs.

10. What if Isabella is left behind and can't find her way home?

War, Politics and Religion

Early critics complained that Austen ignored significant issues and events of her day which encompassed years of war, political upheaval and religious agitation. Recent readers, however, have been more discerning, noticing a feel to the stories and odd comments in her letters that indicate an awareness with which she was not credited in the past.

Fanny's brother, William (*MP*) and the naval figures in *Persuasion* would be reminders of the Wars. Moving the militia from Meryton to Brighton (*P & P*) indicated a knowledge of the army readying itself for embarkation to fight Napoleon. In 1813, Jane writes of a son buried with military honours; in 1814, she refers to Mr Barlow who said that Peace was generally expected, and she speculates on War in America with its political implications. There are also two well-known references to the death of Sir John Moore at Corunna. The conflict between Edmund and Mary (*MP*) would remind the reader of pluralism, Methodism, the rise of Evangelicals—issues that were making such a stir in all parishes. Politics did not seem to interest or have the same impact on Austen and only a small reference is made to Parliament when Edward declares that he is not the right person for that sort of career (*S & S*). Politics in publication was in fact, following the manners of the time: a dangerous subject to approach as it could be seen as disloyalty to the Crown. Authority was sensitive to anything that might cause unrest or spying for the enemy. The Radical Thomas Paine, arrested in France, was not the only one to be thrown into gaol. His *Rights of Man* caused quite a stir although Mary Wollstonecraft's *Vindication of the Rights of Women* was better received. However, politics was best left alone.

In her personal life, Jane Austen was well aware of newsworthy events. Warren Hastings was a family friend. The Austens were naturally very interested in the outcome of his impeachment. The husband of cousin Eliza was guillotined. The fact that two of her brothers were in the Royal Navy fighting for their country gave Jane a comprehensive knowledge of the Napoleonic War at sea and Henry was in the militia which was also pertinent. Her cousin Edward Cooper subscribed to Evangelicalism.

Army	Charles	conflict	Cooper	Eliza
Fencibles	France	Francis	guillotine	Hastings
Henry	militia	Napoleon	navy	parliament
Pitt	revolution	taxes	unrest	Wellington

1. Mr Wickham's drinking habit was a concern, but he always promised that he would stop it tomorrow.
2. The clever pun restored his reputation as a man of discerning grammar.
3. Southcliff ran central to the strategy, and they were confident of success.
4. First Patrick and then Ryan argued the Irish corner and very nearly won the day.

5. The Reverend George Austen roped uprights together and then a pole on the top of the structure completed it so that a sheet could be draped across and make a splendid tent in which his children may shelter and play.

6. There was a big swarm yesterday, but Sir William East located the queen bee and removed her and the swarm from the apple tree before transferring them into his vacant hive.

7. The use of the Italian Enrico operating as a stagehand as well as a tenor saved the show.

8. The red-hot axe severed the bull's head in one fell swoop of the slaughterer's two arms.

9. The monk from Cardiff ran Cistercian monasteries with an efficiency to be admired by any who came to enquire.

10. When I took the children to the menagerie and the cause of a commotion appeared to be a camel, I zapped it with a blow to its behind, threw a blanket over its head and it dropped to its knees.

Dress

A good way to determine the costume worn in England during Jane Austen's lifetime is to have a good look at contemporary art. In 1775, the year of Jane's birth, fashion for ladies included gowns nipped in at the waist, low necklines, long or elbow-length sleeves with flamboyant, wide skirts. Thomas Gainsborough was at the height of his fame. But his paintings were of the nobility and well-off. Jane's mother, before she married, would have been familiar with and probably wore such dresses, of heavy silk or linen. Joshua Reynolds was also exhibiting during Jane's lifetime. On the other hand, William Hogarth (who died in 1764) paints a different portrait. JMW Turner was born the same year as Jane Austen and his paintings reflect fashion in all walks of life.

There were many circumstances at work, however, that would drastically change fashion, not in just women's dress, but everyone's hairstyles, headgear and jackets, cloaks and overcoats. The industrial revolution in the manufacturing of the material enabled faster and cheaper methods to produce cloth from Kay's flying shuttle, the Spinning Jenny of Hargreaves, Arkwright's water loom and Compton's mule to Cartwright's power loom. There was also the advent of cheap raw materials. The local wool and silk from the east were rivalled by cotton that was pouring in from the third side of the slave trade triangle. Cheaper materials brought fashion to the lower middle classes. Our relationship with India heralded the importation of muslins, Kashmir and beautiful shawls.

At the same time, the production and wearing of wigs disappeared altogether. All wigs needed powder and the main ingredient of this was flour. Disastrous harvests in the 1790s and embargoes due to wars with France made the raw ingredients difficult to buy and the prices rose. However, wigs were still being worn in the 1790s, so William Pitt introduced a powder tax. Meanwhile, some men were dispensing with wigs and having their hair shorn. This cutting of the hair was a sympathetic gesture in support of the guillotined French.

Travel restrictions in France brought an interest in the classical forms of Greece and Italy; Egypt also had its influence. And so, the Regency style evolved.

Amber	bonnet	cocquelicot	cravat	gown
Greatcoat	hat	jaconet	lace	muslin
Mull	pelisse	petticoat	poplin	powder
Ribbon	sarsenets	potted	sprigged	trimming

1. He realised that acquiring ownership did not necessarily mean that he had control.
2. There was nothing for it but to make the best of a bad job, but Tom Parker would go away with at least his pride intact.
3. It must not become a whim, us lingering in this way, but perhaps a more definite approach would bring a positive result.

4. The Gardiner children were again blowing bubbles and the sound of a gentle pop linked the present with Jane's memory from long ago.

5. Selina was adamant that she could spot tedious people as soon as they walked into the room and would steer her friend into more lively company.

6. Martha wiped the jampot rim, mingling soap in warm water to ensure that a clean jar was in readiness for the blackberry jam when it had boiled for a sufficient length of time.

7. Discovering the hub on networking the organisation of the protesting millworkers, he thought perhaps he had solved the mystery of their success.

8. A plate of tasty rib bones accompanied the thick steaming soup and a newly baked cottage loaf, helped down with a tankard of ale, set Sidney up for a pleasant evening.

9. If you think that I am bereft of all indifference then you have sadly misunderstood my feelings.

10. It was indeed a muntjac on eternal wonderings though the Rushworth's estate causing untold damage as it munched and meandered its way from one boundary to another and even the ha-ha didn't stop it.

Accomplishments and Virtues

How did these young ladies acquire their accomplishments and what were they?

For the very rich, it was a simple matter of employing a governess. Less well-off families who had a regular income had a choice of peripatetic tutors or suitably accomplished mothers. Jane Austen learnt to play the piano from a tutor who visited the house. Her proficiency came from regular practice, usually before breakfast. Perhaps Cassandra also had piano lessons although she shone in drawing; maybe, also, learning from a peripatetic tutor or at school. For some lucky girls, tutors would be employed for singing lessons, although in towns and cities such as Bath, the young ladies would go to the tutor's studio to learn. Niece Fanny Knight learnt to play the harp. Mary Crawford (*MP*) and the Musgrove sisters (*P*) played the harp. Another avenue for learning accomplishments was a school for young ladies. Jane and Cassandra learnt French at Reading Girls School, no doubt with extra help from Mrs Austen. Maybe, Mr Austen also had a hand in teaching Jane, at least some French and a smattering of Latin. Jane also knew some Italian which she may have picked up through her reading or singing. Dancing was another accomplishment that could be learnt at home. Jane and Cassandra, no doubt, already had some skill at dancing before they learnt more at Reading School. New dances, such as the waltz may require lessons away from these sources. When first introduced in 1813, the waltz caused a sensation, but I can just imagine Jane enjoying it.

Sewing was a necessary accomplishment if you were in the middle-income bracket. The Austen ladies sewed their men's shirts and were capable of altering their clothes. The construction of reticules, decoupage and netting were skills that some girls enjoyed as well as making changes to bonnets and accessories to make them more fashionable. These are all practical accomplishments, but embroidery was also necessary for a young lady to be able to exhibit. In the end, the quality and scope of a young lady's accomplishments depended on a natural aptitude or the amount of practice she was willing to do to improve her ability.

The aim was to present herself as a desirable wife.

Beauty	charm	decorum	dancing	drawing
Elegance	eloquence	grace	health	honour
Humour	musicality	perseverance	poise	punctuality
Reading	sentiment	sensibility	singing	sewing

1. Robert poured the brandy shots in gin glasses and hoped that no one would complain.
2. Anne was forced to withdraw in gathering alarm, wondering where on earth she could retreat to next without being discovered in her agitation at the appearance of Frederick Wentworth in the salon.

3. She knew that It didn't matter which arm was presented, the cowpox injection urged upon her by Mrs Lefroy, was going to hurt.
4. Maria enjoyed all of the running races even though she often came last.
5. Eleanor was an acknowledged connoisseur of furnishings and had spoken about décor umpteen times but the last was always as fresh as the first.
6. The Radical stood on his soapbox speaking in a convincing rhetoric and it was a pure ad in getting them to listen and learn for future enlightenment.
7. Edward took his son George to the lathe although he was still rather young and small to be able to work it by himself.
8. We had to tackle this wearying marathon ourselves, but it was with a great sense of achievement when every article of clothing that we had made was sold and our coffers once more fit to support us.
9. To begin with, the rewards will be small, but you will, in the next phase, win great accolades.
10. It was Christmas and so Sally and I joined the choir to hum our background accompaniment to their sopranos, contraltos and tenors.

Pastimes and Entertainment

Darkness restricted activity because the lighting was by a candle.

There is no record of how old Jane was when she learnt to read but from that day to the end of her life, reading was central to her free hours. It appears that her reading aloud came to life when she could use her voice (including accents) to dramatic effect. The family were enthusiasts of wordplay. They invented rhymes and conundrums to pass travelling time and for entertainment at home. Jane included this pastime to great effect in *Emma*. The Austens enjoyed charades and for several years, performed plays in their barn. The young members of the family relished country fairs and the men loved going to races—when they weren't hunting, shooting or fishing.

Jane enjoyed playing the piano. Books and sheets of her music have survived, witness to the fact that she was an accomplished pianist and a neat copyist of music manuscripts. Hours were spent in writing letters and walking was also enjoyed—either to shop in the local town of Alton, blackberrying in the lanes of the village or just walking for pleasure with her sister or others. It might be through lanes and over fields close to home, visiting her brother in Godmersham, the streets of Bath, the south coast on holiday or just visiting friends.

Jane loved dancing whether it was at Assemblies in Basingstoke, at balls hosted by the local gentry or dances in places where she stayed or lived—Bath, Southampton, London, for example. The Austens were a cultured family so when Jane stayed with Henry and Eliza in London, she was taken to the theatre, opera, concerts and art galleries. She also went to concerts and the theatre in Bath.

Besides sewing for the family, they also sewed garments for the village poor. The sisters were adept at adapting bonnets, making reticules and decorating shawls. Jane had a reputation for being an accomplished needlewoman. Examples of her exquisite work can be seen at the Jane Austen House Museum. Mrs Austen knitted gloves and garters and they worked with willow. They made a patchwork quilt (also on display) gathering pieces from friends and family. In addition, there are letters that Jane wrote and other examples of her talents. Her writing desk, perhaps an example of her greatest pastime of all, is with the British Library.

Actor	assembly	concert	gallery	harp
Opera	painting	parade	pianoforte	play
Quartet	riding	soiree	spilikins	tatting
Theatre	violin	visiting	walk	whist

1. Mary's performance on the pianoforte would be improved, she thought, with arpeggios, accelerator and allegretto—but the audience were of a different opinion.

2. Francis ran to the Hythe at recession and returned just in time for the last lecture of the day.

3. The apothecary was able to throw alkaline substances into the pot to activate a reasonable result.

4. I fell in the pigsty, so I reeked of manure when I shook hands with the man.

5. Lady Hester Stanhope discovered that it was semi-arid in greater parts of the desert but further south it was mostly sand.

6. Young John Knightley was anxious to show his two pennies at the Highbury baker's and wondered how many sugared buns he could buy with that small fortune.

7. It was the be-bop era of jazz in those days and musically it was a very exciting time despite the restrictions of the war.

8. It certainly looked authentic on certificates that were handwritten before the invention of the typewriter.

9. The great man showed no tact organising such an opulent display in front of the Prince Regent.

10. Mrs Norris was put out at tin guards instead of the usual iron mesh and was in no doubt that they would be useless.

Children

Jane Austen always said that an author should write only about what is familiar. It is not surprising, therefore, that few children feature in her novels. Often, they are unattractive— Fanny Price's siblings (*MP*), the Musgroves (*P*) and Middletons (*S & S*). Occasionally they are used to move the plot on, as in the case of *The Watsons* when a side of Emma's personality is revealed when she dances with a disappointed ten-year-old. The number of children allotted to the families in Austen's novels ranges from 2 (Palmers *S & S*, Musgroves *P*) to 10 (Morlands *NA*).

Unfamiliarity or lack of understanding came from not being a parent. However, both Jane and her sister, Cassandra, were devoted and proud aunts and their affection was returned. Jane was amused by their manners and foibles. but was not, in the privacy of letters to her sister, beyond the criticism of bad parenting. (She hoped that one nephew was given 'a wholesome thump or two'). *Sense and Sensibility* included several incidents and shows that Jane must have observed such behaviour and how it was dealt with. Some of her nephews and nieces are mentioned in her Letters: Frank's daughter suffers from seasickness, she takes Edward's two sons rowing on the River Itchen. The Knight children go to the dentist. In Le Faye's published *Letters,* they include some that Jane wrote to her nieces and nephews.

Fond of childhood games, Jane was an excellent bilbo catcher (there's a set at her House Museum in Chawton where you can test your skill and at ninepins which Jane often played). She was, apparently, an excellent player of spillikins. Once, she wrote a Happy New Year letter to her niece, Cassandra-Esten, daughter of brother Charles, with every word written backwards. She sent drawings to 'little Dordy' (George Knight).

As they grew into teenage years, some of her young relations came to her for advice about their writing and Fanny about her love life. In after years, nieces told of stories that their Aunt Jane invented for them. A fond nephew himself, James Edward Austen-Leigh's memoir relied heavily on the memory of the nephews and nieces who could recount anecdotes that reveal part of Jane Austin's character.

Anna	Charles	Edward	Elliot	Fanny
Gardiner	George	Harriet	Harville	John
Mary	Middleton	Morland	Palmer	Price
Richard	Sally	Susan	Walter	William

1. We are fortunate to live in town because it gives us an advantage when shopping for almost everything.
2. Because the captain grew ill, I amputated his foot as it had become gangrenous and would have caused his death.
3. As to regard in errors of etiquette, the two younger Bennet girls were forever committing them much to Jane and Lizzy's chagrin.

4. For Cassandra to wait for the carriage would mean narrowly missing an opportunity to meet with her niece so she walked the short distance between the two houses.

5. If Henry did not steady the fulcrum or land a fish with his hand-held rod there would be no dinner tonight.

6. Mark me well, I otherwise may refuse to endorse your application as tutor to Sir John's sons.

7. "I am not sure your pal merits such devotion Henry," said his father, "because every time you are together, you end up in trouble."

8. Just because Miss Bates may be a bit eccentric, hardly anyone took notice of her funny little ways.

9. It was all your own fault, Lydia.

10. Catherine was uncertain whether to put the injured bird in a cage or get a box which would be warmer and she could always pierce the lid to allow it to breathe.

Status

George, a clever pupil, won a scholarship to St John's College, Oxford. A natural teacher, he returned to the school as a tutor. The sudden death of a Head who had expected George to succeed him, resulted in the Governors appointing another. George returned to Oxford and took Holy Orders. He was gifted Deane and Steventon Livings by a distant, rich cousin. As his representative, George was accepted into a higher rank of society than he would otherwise have expected. His wife, Cassandra Leigh came from nobility. The Leigh's were titled and her grandfather married the sister of the 2nd Duke of Chandos.

However, the family's fortunes were governed by a low income received from the stipends, the tithes and a small farm, supplemented by Mr Austen's paying pupils. Although not well-off, they were respectable and could afford servants and a man to help with the farm. For a year or two, they owned a carriage until William Pitt's tax put a stop to that.

The sons achieved their own status. James became a clergyman and his son, also a clergyman, inherited the Leigh-Perrot fortune. Charles and Francis had successful careers in the navy. Henry entered the militia, became a Land Tax Collector, owned a bank and eventually became a clergyman.

Edward was adopted by very rich cousins called Knight. When Cassandra's fiancé died, he willed her £1,000 and she remained single for the rest of her life as did Jane. Mrs Austen had a small annuity. After Mr Austen died the three women relied on contributions from the sons. Neither of the girls took up the option of teaching. In *The Watsons,* Jane Austen has Charlotte declaring that it would be the last thing she would do. Jane, of course, eventually received money from her publications. When Cassandra was living alone, she did teach a few local pupils for a while.

To summarise, the Austen family hovered on the edge of the upper classes: respectable, intelligent and destined to become the newly emerging upper middle classes or above in some cases.

As for the characters in Austen's novels, it is clear that she favours the navy over the army, nearly every novel has a clergyman in it and few of the title upper class emerge as hero or heroine. Even Darcy, rich as he is, is plain Mister.

Admiral	baron	baronet	captain	clergyman
Colonel	count	curate	Dowager	evangelist
General	gentleman	Lady	lieutenant	Lord
Missionary	preacher	Prince	Reverend	Sir

1. Be sure that it will occur at every corner of Mansfield Park until proper measures are put into place.
2. Catherine's brother, George Morland, was only a lad yet his achievements were quite incredible.
3. Henry jumped over the bar onto the grass beyond and then raced to the road for help.
4. Marco, lonely and listless, put his head in his hands and prayed that someone would come to his rescue.

5. It was a good idea to briefly stop, reach Ermine Street and then take his bearings from there.

6. Edward Knight's plan was to endow age-related persons with a pension appropriate to their status and length of service.

7. Charlotte had to pull or drag the box over to her grandmother so that she could inspect the contents.

8. It was a smidgen era, literally a small, unimportant one that was sandwiched between two great geological ages.

9. Bring thine petty fiasco unto mine own house to receive my forgiving blessing for erring and go thy way in peace to make good thine mistakes.

10. "The Rev, Angel, is true to his calling," said the disrespectful Mary Crawford to her closest friend, "and his is the last profession into which I would marry."

Position in Society

Born into a rich family with a title your inheritance depended on whether you were the first male, otherwise, you were the recipient of an army commission, ordained or studied the law. Politics was automatic if you were titled and an option if you weren't. To be provided for, females depended on marriage unless relations took them in or, awful thought, become `a companion or a governess.

You may be in trade in a country booming in an industrial revolution where there were plenty of manufacturers who were rich but not always accepted by the Aristocracy. Trade also encompassed shopkeepers and artisans. Farmers came somewhere between the two and could be Gentlemen like Mr Austen, Yeomen like the Hayters (*P*) or a tenant like Mr Martin (*E*) The medical profession were indeterminate in their status. We hear of Royal Surgeons who were respected and charlatan apothecaries who were not because of their questionable remedies. Some climbed the status ladder as illustrated by Mr Perry. (*E*)

All of the above needed workers so we find servants in households and labourers on the land. There was a hierarchy here too. These people worked long, hard hours and were paid very little. During Jane's lifetime, both men and women who earned their wages by working for other people were gradually drawn into the expanding towns to become factory workers driven to death by the conditions but were paid more than an agricultural labourer who was often out of work. (See *North and South* by Elizabeth Gaskill)

Press gangs snatched men for the navy and some men volunteered. They volunteered for the army too. At least you were fed and eventually paid. In 1815, after Waterloo, the country saw many of these servicemen—often disabled—on the streets begging. Conditions for the poor were horrendous and beggars and down-and-outs were a common sight. If you were respectable poor and were lucky you lived near to people like the Austens who could help you out. (See also *Lark Rise to Candleford*). Lady Catherine de Bourgh 'manages' the poor in her manor (*P & P*).

Many trades and professions are mentioned in Austen's books and servants are often named.

Andrew	apothecary	baker	butcher	coachman
Doctor	driver	groom	housekeeper	James
Jemima	maid	Martin	nurse	physician
Sam	servant	surgeon	valet	William

1. Mary took the food into the dining room and then took the dirty dishes out to the kitchen.
2. "Take the clock to the window where you can see Betsy," said Mrs Austen, "and rewind it but not too tight on the spring."
3. The gold was to be found on the bottom of a pebble and sand riverbed, but it took a long and tedious time to sort it from the gravel.

4. It was Charles who gave Cassandra and Jane the oval etchings and Francis was the source of the amber necklaces.

5. The top of the hill brought the regiment to a wiser vantage point than lower down where they would not have been able to see the enemy.

6. Sarah opened a market stall as there was an upsurge on the sales of wool and embroidery thread.

7. "Discard the weaklings, Mr Collins," advised Lady de Bourgh, "but cherish those who show promise."

8. "I do love to add jam, especially when it is spread on a scone before adding clotted cream and a fresh strawberry," declared Mrs Elton.

9. "Oh, Ma, I didn't do it," he said, "and please don't blame me for the pig escaping either."

10. Take your horse to the mart in Tattersalls because that is where the best deals are to be found.

Food and Drink

Water was often impure so many of all classes drank alcoholic drinks instead. Pumps headed wells but the purity of the water was not guaranteed. If you lived in the country then you may have access to fresh milk, even, like Mrs Austen, own an Alderney. But the milk for sale in towns carried by milkmaids was often tainted before it was sold. Food and drink left a lot to be desired and you needed a strong constitution to survive, especially if you were poor. Food was often adulterated. For example, chalk and alum were the norm but lime, ground animal bones and even white lead were suspected to be added to bread. Preservation by salting, smoking or pickling was a regular strategy to keep food through the winter or to prevent it from going bad. Herbs and spices disguised much of the taste of stale or even rotten food. Ice houses, owned by the rich, were used mostly only for that.

Spices and some fruits such as oranges, dates and raisins had long been known in the country; potatoes and turkeys were now well established, but pineapples were rare on the Regency table. Macaroni from Italy and tomatoes were the new imports. French cuisine had grown in reputation, but it was roast beef and boiled cabbage that pleased the English palate.

Mrs Austen took care of the kitchen garden. Besides her cow, she kept ducks, chickens, guineafowl and turkeys. Vegetables were grown and Casandra kept bees for honey used for sweetening and making mead. There were fruit trees, gooseberries and strawberries. They no doubt gathered nuts, blackberries, elderflower and mushrooms. Pork and mutton came from the farm and the men provided game and rabbit. Some women kept a household book and that of Martha Lloyd (the friend who lived for many years with the Austen ladies) can be seen at Jane Austen House Museum. We learn of Jane's responsibilities from her letters and the occasions when she had to take on more in Cassandra's absence. They sometimes went out to dine and occasionally entertained family or friends.

Food, drink, meals occur frequently in the novels. Mrs Bennet entertained Mr Darcy to dinner (*P & P*), Catherine Morland was served tea in posh china (*NA*) and Emma disgraced herself at the picnic on Box Hill (*E*).

Apples	butter	cabbage	cocoa	Constantia
dinner	gruel	Madeira	mutton	Negus
nutmeg	pork	rhubarb	soup	strawberries
supper	tea	toast	vegetables	wine

1. "Nuts, any nuts," Mrs Elton complained, "even if I eat just one single chestnut, megrim will surely follow and keep me in bed for days on end."
2. Whatever you need or have, get a blessed grasp on your bearings before setting out, as I don't want a message to say that you are without some essential or other.

3. Thorpe was determined to win, stuffing his mouth with as much as he could manage which was a test early on in the competition to see who could eat the most meat pies.

4. It was dark above the stairs but there seemed to be no threat and Henry Tilney had gone to Woodston, so up Catherine went albeit rather nervously.

5. Mrs Bennet had not believed in nervous complaints of others but was profuse in declaring her own.

6. It is all very well to make things difficult but termly tests is taking it a bit too far.

7. Little Harry was not averse to a thump or kick and thought a pinch now and then would gain attention.

8. The farmer with his wagon is a kindly soul and thus usually picks up persons who are walking to market and takes not a penny for his troubles.

9. Francis pulled hard on the oars in an effort to get to a stable mooring on the River Itchen where he could tie up his boat for the night.

10. Catherine went below in evermore hesitating steps, worried what she would find in the cellar.

Medical

There was much irritating illness within Jane's own family, illnesses that these days could be cured by a visit to a pharmacist or doctor. The strides made in identifying, alleviating and curing certain complaints since Jane's death in 1817 is phenomenal.

The Reverend George Austen appears to have been a fit and healthy man. We hear of no complaints, either physical or verbal until the last few days of his life when death came quickly and unexpectedly. On the other hand, if one is to believe completely in Jane's reports, Mrs Austen was a 'martyr to complaints'. She was once treated with leeches. It appears that she suffered from travel sickness for which she took bitters. and who can wonder at the weakening of a woman's body after giving birth to eight children, running a household, not just for the family but for the addition of several resident boys? The task of managing domestic animals and a vegetable garden was not easy. Mr Lyford prescribed laudanum. No, we can forgive her for her need for laudanum and other medicines. Once she wrote an amusing poem after 'cheating death'. But Jane was always sceptical and derisory about her mother's constant complaints of feeling ill.

James suffered much illness at the end of his life, Edward had stomach problems and gout (for which he sought relief in Bath), Henry had bouts of illness and nearly died. George, the second son, had disability problems. Charles died from cholera aboard ship and is buried in Trincomalee. Until the end of her life, however, Cassandra seems to have taken after her father in good health. Frank outlived them all and died when he was ninety-one years old.

Jane, we know, was a mere forty-one when she died from an unidentified condition although some believe it was Addison's disease.

There is not a lot of illness or accidents in Jane Austen's novels. There is Marianne's near death, of course (*S & S*) and the apothecary friend of Mr Woodhouse (*E*), Mrs Bennet suffers from her nerves (*P & P*), Tom Bertram has a severe illness through excessive drinking (*MP*), but most are to be found in *Sanditon* which begins with an accident to a coach. We are quickly introduced to the Parkers who appear to be hypochondriacs.

Accident	apothecary	bile	bruise	complaint
Cough	disease	disorder	doctor	fainting
Fits	injury	invalid	leech	physician
pills	sprain	surgeon	swoon	tonic

1. It was perfectly alright to conjoin valid situations providing they did not interfere with the general run of things.
2. Caroline Bingley was determined to equip ill-serving members with permission-to-leave cards as soon as possible.

3. Robert admitted that it is impossible to grasp rainbows and there certainly isn't a pot of gold at the end.

4. My dear, you must wear it if it suits you but don't blame me if it turns out to be wrong for the occasion.

5. Take it from me, the Pontiff ain't in gorgeous robes because he is showing off but because they are the traditional garb of his station.

6. The gang make their way along the narrow path as the guides urge on the need to make haste which does not threaten their safety in any way.

7. It wasn't everyone's idea to nick the old hag's book but certainly, most of the class thought it would be fun to hide it from her.

8. The nettles stung Lizzy's ankle, so she found the leaf of a doc to reduce the uncomfortable, stinging itch where great white bumps were appearing.

9. It was imperative that they flee, chasing the departing chaise that might leave without their rescue.

10. The young gentleman's idea was to press, woo, nurture then declare his love for the beautiful daughter of Lord Mansfield.

Buildings

Jane was born in a large, dilapidated rectory in Steventon, later replaced on another site so there is barely a footprint of the house where she was born. An archaeological dig has revealed very little.

When Mr Austen took his three women to Bath, they lived in a terrace house. After his death, the ladies went to live in brother Frank's house in Southampton, keeping his wife company whilst he was at sea. The advantage of this house was the garden which they had very much missed in Bath.

They stayed there from 1806 until 1809 but Frank's family was growing and it was necessary to find other accommodation. Edward Austen Knight offered them a cottage and they chose the one in Chawton. Hampshire was their favourite county so they would return to an area where they knew many residents. In Austen's day, cottages were very different from what we know as a cottage today. There were six bedchambers and garrets for storage and servants.

Besides the houses in which she lived, Jane also stayed and visited great country houses—Godmersham and Adlestrop for instance. She went out to take tea, to dine and to dance in many grand houses. Once, she visited the ancestral home of the Leighs, Stoneleigh Abbey, the greatest of them all.

When Henry took up residence in London there was no need for hotels, although his place in Chelsea was still in the countryside. Travelling meant a change of horses or even an overnight stay in an inn. One of the earliest changes of abode for Jane was the school in Reading which was situated in the Abbey gatehouse.

Jane, then, was familiar with the best of town and country but she was also familiar with the humble homes of the less fortunate as she often visited the poor in both villages of Steventon and Chawton.

In her novels, Austen rarely describes a building apart from Northanger Abbey, but the names that she gives them would indicate to her readers what to expect: Donwell and Northanger Abbey, Mansfield and Netherfield Park and just by calling them by a given name—Pemberley—indicates a building of respectability and wealth.

Abbey	barn	castle	cottage	farmhouse
Hall	hotel	house	hovel	inn
Lodge	lodgings	mansion	manor	parsonage
Seminary	school	shop	stables	terrace

1. She realised in the end that even if she ran a faster race, she would never beat her rival to the winning posts.

2. "Ma'am," said he in a superior voice, "if lobster is beyond your purse, then let crab be your choice." And the poor woman turned her head in embarrassment.

3. Kitty and Lydia giggled their way to Meryton, determined to find a handsome man or in any event,

a man who was not bad looking with whom to flirt and dance.

4. The echo velocity of the yodelling in the valley was beyond any sound experienced by Edward Knight on his Grand Tour.

5. Jane found the children and then took them home with all the berries and scratches that they had collected.

6. Directing the servants, Mrs Norris told them, "After inspecting the wainscot, tag every piece of furniture that is to be removed from this room."

7. Miss Bates was bandaged from toes to ankle after she had carelessly picked up a hot, elderly saucepan and dropped it onto her foot when the handle finally parted company.

8. Henry was keen to be introduced to the girl as soon as she entered the room and was in nervous anticipation as the means soon presented itself.

9. In my young days, the choice was hopscotch, skipping or spinning a top, none of these silly rhymes whilst clapping hands or touching toes.

10. Marianne was despondent and cast leaf after leaf into the stream watching them float away, just like the dreams that she now realised would come to nothing.

The Picturesque and Landscape Gardening

Henry Austen added a biographical notice to *Persuasion* and *Northanger Abbey*: "At a very early age she was enamoured of Gilpin on the Picturesque." Jane enjoyed rural scenes (Fanny Price {*MP*} speaks for her, verdure is appreciated in *Emma*), but she was not beyond satirising the picturesque. An early example is in her *History of England*: "…nothing can be said in his [Henry VIII] vindication, but that his abolishing religious Houses & leaving them to the ruinous depredations of time has been of infinite use to the landscape of England." Knowledge of the Picturesque comes when the Tilneys explain it to Catherine Morland and Blaise Cattle, which John Thorpe planned to visit, is a folly. (*NA*) The picturesque is also featured when Marianne (for) and Edward (against) discuss its merits (*S & S*). Published in 1809, *The Tour of Dr Syntax in search of the Picturesque* is about a rural schoolmaster-pastor. In attempting to make his fortune with an illustrated travel book, he manages only to sketch a dilapidated signpost and invents its picturesque requirements. Full of misadventures, his book featuring the picturesque never materialises. Jane Austen would have loved the irony in it.

The two notable landscape architects of the time were Capability Brown and Humphry Repton. There is no specific reference to Lancelot Brown in the novels—he opened up the landscape and planted clumps of trees—although there is a hint of it at Pemberley (*P & P*) which perhaps gives some readers the idea that it is modelled on Chatsworth. Brown was fond of adding temples (there is one at Godmersham) and follies. He also designed Nuneham Courtney for Lord Harcourt and the village stood in the way, so he got rid of it. Oliver Goldsmith wrote *The Deserted Village* in protest of this common practice at the time (1770). Jane Austen uses the name Harcourt disparagingly in her Juvenilia.

Humphry Repton was born later and he called himself a 'landscape gardener' indicating his canvas to be somewhat smaller than Brown's. Austen was familiar with his work as he had landscaped the Leigh's Manor garden at Adlestrop including adding water features. Repton is mentioned by Henry Crawford (*MP*) when the family visit Sotherton.

Adlestrop	Blaise	Brown	Catherine	Crawford
Edward	folly	Gilpin	Goldsmith	ha-ha
Harcourt	Marianne	perspective	Picturesque	Repton
Ruins	Sotherton	Syntax	temple	Tilney

1. Marianne's psyche was manic, raw for days on end, and no one but Elinor could soothe or help her through the days and nights.
2. It was the fourth arc our triumphant forbears declared the best decorated of the six that formed the bridge over the river.

3. Not quite a Nabob, Rowntree was nevertheless a tremendous contributor to the welfare of his people and to the community in general.
4. "It is Sarah! Aha, we have caught you in the act, you thieving little beggar," exclaimed Thorpe as he grabbed her ear and dragged her out of the pantry.
5. It is thus, so the R to number 6 in S row keeps the Robinsons away from the Steeles.
6. Only one more item, please, as we must not overload the donkey cart.
7. Slowly the cat advanced and crept on ever closer to her prey, paused and then pounced.
8. There is no use taking old Smith at his word for he is most unreliable.
9. She was histrionic at her inexperience in the matter and therefore her judgement was in question.
10. Sally must read lest Roper gets ideas about his sister taking over the task of entertaining Lady Dalrymple.

Transport and Travel

Contrary to general belief, Jane Austen was not a lady who stayed at home to write novels in a country cottage.

Jane was young when she was taken from Hampshire to Kent, via London, to visit Mr Austen's relations. She went to school in Oxford and Reading, Berks, and visited Bath (Som) frequently. In 1798/9, she went with her mother and sister to Henley in Oxfordshire. In 1806, she visited the Leighs in Adlestrop, Glos and stayed in Lichfield, Staffs when she visited Stoneleigh Abbey in Warw. London was a frequent destination during Austen's publishing years. taking the best part of the day to travel, breaking for repast and change of horses.

When living in Bath the Austens took annual holidays to the coasts of Dorset and Devon for example; mention was made of a proposed visit to Barry in Wales. In 1804, the ladies went to Worthing, West Sussex, and when Jane was unwell, she and Cassandra went to Cheltenham Spa, Glos, to take the waters. She probably visited the Isle of Wight when they lived in Southampton, Hants.

With all this travel, how did she get around? We know from her letters that she travelled (accompanied) by both post and stagecoach. Sometimes, she was lucky enough to travel in a private coach—her brothers Henry and Edward both owned their own and so did her father for a couple of years. She used a Sedan Chair and rode in a phaeton with Mr Evelyn. Brother Henry rode many miles on his horse, but Jane was not a rider. Jane used the ferry at Southampton. She moved around her locality on foot. The sisters travelled by donkey cart to shops in Alton and Farringdon and when her illness prevented walking, Jane rode the donkey.

Some Turnpike Trusts maintained their stretch of the road well or adequately. Macadamising did not make an impression until just after Austen's death. The Bath Road (now the A4) was the best in the country. Rivers were used more for transporting goods than pleasure. One of her letters tells that she rowed on the River Itchen with her nephew when they stayed with her in Southampton. Portsmouth was where Jane might see her brothers' ships.

Travel features in all of Austen's novels and she uses the names of her brother's ships (with their permission) in two of them.

HMS Asp	barouche	carriage	cart	chaise
Coach	curricle	HMS Elephant	equipage	gig
HMS Grappler	hack	horse	HMS Laconia	landau
HMS Leopard	phaeton	post	ship	stage

1. He drove the donkey from Ravenscar to the countryside trusting that the parcels were securely tied to the panniers.

2. It was unnecessary to throw such an obvious, less than subtle quip agents were sure to dislike and thus lessen the possibility of being chosen.

3. Henry Tilney selected the venue carefully as he wanted it to be a special treat for their honeymoon.

4. They would condemn her anyway whether it was for being a witch or several counts of treachery.

5. Returning from India, using the vernacular, both Philadelphia and Eliza Hancock declared that a cup of cha is every bit a drink to be savoured as any other beverage in England.

6. Now, wouldn't that be an achievement—to land a unicorn or catch a griffin?

7. It was a matter of choice whether he would jump ostensibly into the fray or stand back and let others do so.

8. Not just a gentleman, my dear, but a rich gentleman to boot so make sure that you dress appropriately and mind your manners.

9. If it wasn't a tele-phantom for their next theatricals, then it was something queer going on in the barn like a villager playing the fool.

10. To give Denny and co a chance to make good their mistake was probably the best way forward.

The Thames Valley

Jane Austen and her family's connection with the Thames Valley has long been neglected, the places and circumstances skimmed over or hardly mentioned. Some, such as Jon Spence (*Becoming Jane Austen*), work on perfectly plausible assumptions: if Jane was at school with her cousin Jane Cooper whose father was the incumbent at Sonning just down the road from Reading, then Jane must have visited him there. However, there is no evidence to support this. Nor is there any evidence that Jane visited her Uncle James Leigh Perrot at Scarlets, near Wargrave, just a little further on along the Bath Road. They may have conveyed the girls between Reading and Steventon where they visited from time to time. Gilbert East (Mr Austen's pupil) lived at Hurley, a few miles from Henley.

Phyllis Court in Henley was the home of the Coopers where local families met—the Leighs, Powys', East's, Newell's (Mrs Birch) and perhaps their university friend George Austen.

Some letters tell us that Jane, Cassandra and Mrs Austen visited Edward Cooper then curate at Harpsden (near Henley where Mrs Austen's father had been rector and where she was born). The diary of Mrs Caroline Powys (a close friend of Mrs

Austen) tells us that she entertained Jane and her sister at Fawley, a village on the Marlow side of Henley, during this same visit in 1798. Jane was in Henley again in 1813 when Henry was on a Land Tax collecting mission. They had overnighted at Windsor and on their way to Chawton, although Jane feared that she would not get any further than Reading that day.

Going further west on the Oxford Road (present-day A329) from Reading we pass through Purley and reach Basildon. Basildon Park was built by Sir Francis Sykes when he returned from India. A friend of Warren Hastings, he brought Hastings' sickly boy to England for his health's sake and to be educated. The child was handed over to Mr and Mrs George Austen. Awaiting his trial, Hastings stayed briefly at Purley Hall, neighbouring Basildon Park and close to many returnees from India in the area. Perhaps Henry rode over to visit him there. Basildon Park was, of course, Netherfield in *Pride and Prejudice* featuring Keira Knightley and Matthew Macfadyen.

Basildon	(Mrs) Birch	Caroline	Cooper	Fawley
Harpsden	Hastings	Henley	Hurley	Leigh
Phyllis (Court)	Powys	Purley	Reading	Scarlets
School	Sonning	Sykes	Thames	Wargrave

1. The sassy kestrel hovered above its prey, at an unbelievable height, before swooping down upon the unfortunate animal below.
2. The Sharps denied all knowledge of the people and declared that they had never visited anywhere near where they lived.

3.   If we go to war, grave outcomes are inevitable.

4.   It was a surprise to the Highbury residents when ley-lines crossed two sides of the village.

5.   Trevithick's car let several daring people experience a ride in it as it was drawn by his noisy iron engine along a Cornish street.

6.   Charles bent down to scoop Ermintrude the escapist chicken up into his arms and quickly dispatched the hen by wringing her neck.

7.   In their old age, Mr and Mrs George Austen could recall eight children who, like any family, had brought them worries but mostly joy and pride.

8.   Thorpe would eat any bread in greedy haste, especially if it was spread with a generous helping of dripping.

9.   He yelled loudly with the intention to spur le Yacine on to a greater victory in the field of combat.

10.   For goodness' sake don't let that ham espy me in the audience because he is sure to overact the mimic.

Oxford

Jane Austen's mother Cassandra Leigh had connections with Oxford. Her Uncle Theophilus Leigh (1691-1785) was Master of Balliol College and a great character. When Cassandra was presented to him as a child, he commended her for her 'sprack wit'. As he was still in post when Jane Austen was in Oxford to be tutored, it is possible that they met and maybe he recognised the Leigh intelligence in her. As an adult, Cassandra Leigh, was often in Oxford and had relations and friends who were students. Tom Powys was a particular friend who may have introduced her to his student friend the 'handsome Proctor'—George Austen.

George had first attended St John's college thanks to a scholarship from Tunbridge School and, as we have seen, after a brief return to the school, went back to St John's. Thus, George's future took an unplanned turn and the rest is history.

The oldest son James and the middle son Henry also attended St John's College through a Founder's Kin scholarship (from the Leigh side). The two boys founded *The Loiterer* in the image of other popular similar magazines. In one edition, there was a letter from a Sophia Sentiment whom some believe to be Jane Austen. If that is so, then James must have dragged the girls around Oxford to show them the venerable buildings which may have included a brief visit to see Great Uncle Theophilus. Eliza Feuillide commented on Henry's fashionable appearance when she visited him and James, declaring a desire to wear an undergraduate cap.

When Rector at Steventon Mr Austen took in boys to tutor for University entry, some of whom were the sons of his fellow Oxford undergraduates. One was the son of William East, Gilbert, who lived in Hall Place, Hurley. Edward Cooper, another university friend, married Cassandra Leigh's sister Jane and it was Edward's sister—Mrs Cawley—who tutored Jane, Cassandra and his daughter His son married into the Powys family and was the curate of Harpsden.

Descendants of the Austens continue to distinguish themselves in the Halls of Oxford University.

Austen	Cassandra	Cawley	Cooper	East
Edward	Henry	James	(Founders) Kin	Leigh
(The) Loiterer	Oxford	Powys	Proctor	Sophia
sprack (wit)	student	Theophilus	Thomas	University

1. Mr Knightley collected the jewellery box for delivering to Emma as soon as he returned from London.

2. Mr Yates hoped to give a sterling performance in their theatricals, but he was caught out by Sir Thomas.

3. The sting of the wasp racked Charlotte's hand for days on end and not even Mr Collins' remedy could ease the pain.

4. The Bennets ended up with twenty pots of jam, especially of blackberry, which accounted for almost half of them.

5. The cricket team will include Theo, Phil, Usama, Kaan and Edward for certain but we still have at least six more members to contact.

6. Mrs Phillips always shopped at the Co-op, ergo a welcome bonus to spend at Christmas.

7. These boxes hold twenty-four examples and are especially designed to be safely transported so phials with the serum must be packed in them and then put into cold storage until collected.

8. "The so-called war department has let us down once again Darcy," Colonel Forster complained, "and I find that the Regiment must remove from Brighton and head to the east coast."

9. Deciding upon a suitable profession for his sons was important to Mr Austen so he sent Frank into the Royal Navy and with that success Charles entered that service also.

10. Sir John Middleton put his horse to stud entirely against the advice of Colonel Brandon.

Bath

Mrs Austen's sister, Jane, married Edward Cooper. The Coopers had two children—Edward and Jane. After Southcote (Reading), Dr Cooper went to reside in Bath where he had another Living. Bath was held in affection by the two families as they and other university friends had frequented the city in its heyday. George Austen and Cassandra Leigh had been wed at Walcott Church where their mutual friend Thomas Powys had officiated. It is likely that the Austens took Cassandra and Jane to visit the Coopers in Bath in the eighteenth century. Mrs Austen's brother James Leigh (to become Leigh-Perrot) and his wife lived in Paragon. Once she went with brother Edward when they stayed in Queen Square. These years seem to have been happy experiences for Jane because out of them came *Susan* (*Northanger Abbey*) Jane's note, when some years later she thought of publication tells the reader that it was written in 'earlier times'.

However, Jane was to live a less happy time there. The move from Steventon was sudden and unexpected, apparently causing Jane distress. They stayed with the Leigh Perrots whilst looking for a house to rent. Although fond of her uncle, Jane did not like her aunt at all. Not a good start. Worse was to come. They had hardly settled in the city (first in Sydney

Place and then Green Park Buildings) when George Austen died. The ladies lived in Gay Street then Trim Street. This rapid decline in fortune ceased when the women went to live in Southampton with Frank.

The unhappy events of the last sojourn in Bath are reflected in *Persuasion* when the heroine, Anne Elliot, is also whisked away to Bath from the only home she had known. There were one or two happy times that relieved the tedium of Bath for Jane: outings and holidays. Jane particularly enjoyed Lyme and it may have been there that she met the young man to whom Cassandra referred. *Persuasion* reflects an unhappy Bath, there unwillingly, a visit to Jane's favourite resort, romance for a woman past her first bloom, an intimate knowledge of the Royal Navy, the solace of poetry. No wonder some people believe that Anne Elliot is really Jane Austen. As we have seen Kipling saw Frederick and Jane in love (*Jane's Marriage*).

Bath	Cassandra	Clifton	cousin	death
Edward	George	James	Jane	Lyme
Outing	(Leigh)Perrot	Persuasion	romance	Southcote
Steventon	sudden	Susan	Thomas	Walcot

1. Mrs Bennet had invited Bingley and Darcy to supper, rotating the seating arrangements from one plan to another before finally settling on the one that placed Darcy furthest away from herself.
2. Jane walked away disappointedly, measuring her steps in a slow retreat from a fruitless visit to the Bingley town residence.

3. The child put a thumb at her mouth, but seeing the disapproving look from her mother, quickly took it away to show that she was not going to suck it.

4. He was neither a judge or germane to the enquiry so Mr Bennet allowed Darcy to deal with the matter as he thought fit.

5. Darcy often went for a ride at his aunt's manor so Lizzy should not have been surprised to see him trotting towards her.

6. The past event on everyone's mind was not one of mutual happiness.

7. The residents at Newal Cottage were a pleasant family whom everyone liked.

8. When Sir Thomas Bertram's chef introduced couscous into the menu it was under the mistaken belief that his master had enjoyed it in Antigua.

9. Her near faint caused him to give her a barbaric lift only out of sheer frustration rather than unkindness.

10. It was fair weather when she left the house but now Marianne was out in gusty wind and the threat of rain.

London

As far as we know, Jane's first visit to London was as a child when her father took some of his family on a visit to his relations in Tonbridge Wells, breaking their journey to Kent in London and staying in a hotel in Cork Street where Mr Austen bought a hat. The Austen men bought their wigs and hats in London.

When Henry Austen took up residence in the city it made life a lot easier for his family. Sometimes, it was a brief stay with him as whoever was visiting were usually en route to visit Edward in Godmersham. During her publishing years, Jane stayed for several weeks at a time so Henry and Eliza gave Jane experiences that she relished and may not otherwise have enjoyed.

A cultural family, there were days when they visited art galleries and evenings when they went to the theatre or opera. Often Henry and Eliza entertained and, in turn, were hosts; Jane was usually included in an invitation when she was there. There were visits, too, to notable places: Astley's and the Liverpool Museum. There were often other relatives staying with Henry. On one occasion, a niece had teeth extractions by Mr Scarman and Jane was persuaded by her nieces; Eliza and Henry, to have her hair arranged by Mr Hall in a modern style—much to her abashed amusement—for a society event. A visit to London, whether just passing through or staying a little bit longer, always included a long shopping list that included items for oneself and one's family. This would include a visit to Grafton House, Bedford House and calling for some of Mr Twining's tea.

Whilst staying with her brother, Jane met a French emigre as well as the Prince Regent's surgeon. The latter was attending Henry who had become very ill resulting in a lengthened stay by Jane to care for him. Discovering her as the author of novels admired by the Prince, the surgeon passed on the information that she was in London resulting in a tour of the library in Carlton House plus the dedication to the Royal Prince in her current book *Emma*. Jane also met up with family friends—the Terry's and the Tilson's.

From the earliest writing of her *Juvenilia,* London is always mentioned and sometimes in detail, illustrating Austen's knowledge of the city and using its environs to establish the characters' personality and status.

Astley's	Carlton (House)	City	Eliza	émigré
Extraction	family	hair	Henry	host
Hotel	gallery	London	publish	Regent
Shopping	surgeon	Terry	theatre	Tilson

1. The worsening of the weather encouraged Lucy's urge onwards towards home at a quickening pace.
2. The child was very distressed until songs sung to her by Nanny soothed her and gradually the crying ceased.

3. Although the situation was chronic, it yet had some benefit in the growing confidence of the man as he overcame his adversity.

4. In their tour of Cornwall, Henry drove her in his carriage all the way to The Lizard and back to Truro for dinner.

5. Lady Lucas did not hold with air balloons and thought Lizzy too daring for wards when she heard that she had ascended in one even though it was safely tethered.

6. When I saw them, I greeted them enthusiastically much to everyone's delight.

7. As the room was so hot Elizabeth dampened down the fire and opened the windows, much to Mrs Bennet's annoyance.

8. What heat remained was sufficient to keep them comfortably warm until it was time for tea.

9. Whoever you call on, do not outstay your welcome, my dear, for it is bad manners for a young lady to do so for longer than twenty minutes.

10. In Bath, both ostlers and stable hands prided themselves on their speed and efficiency when the Stage or Post drew up to the inn.

Solutions

These sentences are inspired by Jane Austen, not written by her.

Jane Austen—A Family Life

1. Mr Darcy's bailiff ran knowing hands down the flanks of the horse before giving his opinion.
2. The handyman went directly to Mr Woodhouse's hencoop, erecting more wire fencing to prevent further attacks by the fox.
3. Mrs Goddard presented the book to her enthralled pupils, who sat in silence as she read in genuine feelings of pathos, anger and joy.
4. Collecting the box for dropping off at the Bates' on the way, Emma put it on the seat beside her and the carriage drove off.
5. The snow on Box Hill provided ample opportunity for the toboggan naturally, but there was insufficient to accommodate anyone on skis.
6. Whatever Edmund said or did for Fanny Price it was always the best even to not sparing the effort required.
7. There was essence of yarrow root in her store, but Mrs Morland gave Catherine the syrup of some tonic

haw to nip the cough in the bud before it affected her chest.

8. It was a question of whether Maria Lucas, Sandra Phillips or Mary King should take the leading role although neither were really good enough for it.

9. With the application of a little rouge or gentle pinching of the cheeks, her pallor would become less evident when she presented herself to the company.

10. If it hadn't been for the theft, the total to naval funds would have been considerably more worthwhile donating.

Sense and Sensibility

1. The agitated warden caused a lot of upset and stress amongst the girls of the Young Ladies Seminary in Richmond.

2. Eleanor Tilney dressed in taste, elegant in her white gown, worn in styles suitable for every occasion.

3. Because of their dreadful grammar, I annexed the whole area until their language was compatible with what was required with the rest of the group.

4. Henry grasped hold of the bar to numb his opponent's arm with a well-aimed hit to the elbow.

5. Edward Knight had become interested in carpentry and particularly enjoyed working on his lathe, so he selected carefully, taking relatively hard ash wood planks from the store in the barn, to make a new leg for the broken chair in the library.

6. It was a difficult manoeuvre as he and his pal merged into the shadows afforded by the rocks, without getting their feet wet.

7. It was a good hotel, in or outside, for the price, and there was no arguing about who went where in the end.

8. She was most upset by the whole affair and neither house nor land would satisfy her, however much money was involved.

9. I think you will, I am sure, want to be involved in the arrangements so that you are satisfied that everything is as you wish.

10. Mr Knightley worked his way through the crowd into the middle to negotiate with the two boys who didn't look as though they would be able to settle their argument without knocking their heads together.

Pride and Prejudice

1. Isabella's eyes sparkled almost as brightly as the lovely diamonds he was about to fasten about her neck.

2. Margaret snatched the ribbon from her sister's hands and offered her thanks with ill grace.

3. Lucy looked at the food on her plate, pushed away the lamb to Nancy and resolved to never eat any red meat ever again.

4. The shawls were piled high—upon shelves already full—on donated and unwanted clothes that might be worth giving to the poor.

5. Charles Bingley adjusted his wife Jane's bonnet, her field of vision thus widened to encompass the complete and unhindered view of their new Staffordshire home that lay before them.

6. The two sisters clung together as the thunderclap hammered their eardrums and the rain-soaked them through to the skin.

7. The boundary took shape as the hardened arc, yet to set thoroughly, gave a pleasant access to the walled garden.

8. It was a great disappointment to the Thorpe family as they walked along Bournemouth high street without finding a single shop that sold hats.

9. Edmund passed the tweezers to Fanny for sterilising in the pan of hot water before extracting the splinter that was just protruding from Susan's finger.

10. "I assure you that the swill I ambushed you with, will not harm you, but might even improver the texture of your skin," laughed John Thorpe as he looked upon his sister's furious countenance.

Mansfield Park

1. He was walking round his plantation with his manager and there, before Sir Thomas Bertram's eyes, was a giant iguana that both frightened and fascinated him.

2. The poor lady ate something that disagreed with her constitution resulting in her death after weeks of suffering.

3. Who cannot but worship ugly ducklings when you know that they will turn into swans?
4. John Thorpe's anger kept him arguing, ranting and generally making himself obnoxious to all and sundry.
5. The leg was too horrific, raw for days after the initial injury and a suppurating mess for weeks afterwards.
6. Religion was supposed to be tolerated in those days tho' Mass had to be observed in secret all the same.
7. She deserves more appreciation for accompanying the woman on her travels but barely a French franc is as much as she can expect for reward.
8. Maria was neither wanton nor rising above her station, but at least deserved a little respect for what she tried to be.
9. They discovered that the Geographical Society only needed mundane adjustments and routine inspections from time to time in order for it to function properly.
10. Henry may go on Monday to Moscow perhaps or if not, it will have to wait until Friday because there are no tickets available from Berlin between those two days.

Emma

1. To receive such esteem made her feel appreciated if only momentarily.
2. In order to reach Bristol, you must travel west on Mr Brunel's train from London and once you get there you will find plenty of cabs to take you to the church.

3. It was carried on well and truly with his interest at heart so, although it was not quite what he had hoped for, he accepted with good grace.

4. Lizzy didn't care a fig for the king's tonnish friend and snapped her fingers in his face even though it might have resulted in social disgrace.

5. Mary gathered the dandelions, chickweed and groundsel in a basket and took it home for her bantams and rabbits.

6. In the evening there was usually at least one bat, especially flying over the Pemberley stream, catching insects that flew above and around the water.

7. If Mr Gardiner didn't find somewhere to lodge or get someone to put him up, he wouldn't be able to go to his trade meeting in Birmingham.

8. James was proud of his Church art, fielding the negative comments with aplomb and accepting the praise, which he felt was due to him, with a nonchalance that said nothing for his modesty.

9. At the Wedgewood warehouse the storeman was instructed to brand all seconds with a different colour to the china that was perfect.

10. The baby had wind, so Rosalie patted it on the back, hoping to calm the child and get rid of the offending disorder before Mr and Mrs Palmer returned.

Persuasion

1. "If you think that wall is too high for me to climb over," said Catherine, "you are very much mistaken and I will prove you wrong this instant."

2. Henry bowled fast and the bat hardly tipped the ball as Frank sent it soaring over beyond the rectory hedge and into the lane.

3. David was destined to become a monk for devious reasons not acknowledged by his stepfather, but he would not submit to such arrogance without protests.

4. Catherine's preference for the Gothic lay in a desire to be knowledgeable rather than eccentric.

5. Edward took hold of the two-pronged pitchfork to pile the hay, terminating his hard work only when all had been gathered and formed a stack that looked as professional as any farm labourer could build.

6. The servants at Purley Hall were astounded as Mr Warren Hastings' kangaroo kept bounding in front of the house for almost an hour until at last it was cornered by the gardener and stableboy to join the other exotic animals kept there by their owner.

7. The physician Tysoe Saul Hancock told the Ranee, "You can give the Raj a message from me and that is I am confirmed in my original opinion."

8. In 1822, when appointed to the Tower of London menagerie, Alfred Cops brought in 300 more animals as the place had gone into decline and he used the walrus' selling power to attract more visitors.

9. To counteract her toothache, Eliza was told to apply mouth-numbing crushed cloves to the offending area.

10. Because of Lady de Bourgh's authoritarianism, it has destroyed the village spirit and made the community resentful.

Northanger Abbey

1. Once arrived at the ball, engaged for every dance, Lydia was a happier young lady than she had been when she set out in such haste.

2. They are usually to be found in Gawsworth or persuade them to go to Macclesfield if that is what you prefer.

3. Whether you like lean or fatty meat is immaterial to the choice available I'm afraid, so we must make the best of a bad meal.

4. Perhaps if you give Sir Thomas a hug, he surely must respond to such an affectionate gesture or else he is too hard hearted for words.

5. She poured more wine, now fuller to nearer the top of the glass, lest she seemed ungenerous.

6. George was relieved to get out of the woods to never return there again without a companion.

7. The Making of Bread Act of 1800 prohibited the miller of Meryton from producing flour other than wholemeal, then rye became a consideration as an addition.

8. So, if Maria is always late, is a bell an answer to the problem or can you think of a better strategy?

9. Mr Darcy was rich, ardently in love with Lizzy and therefore should have assured her of a happy future.

10. If crab be your choice with lobster as another preference, then you cannot do better than visit the island and there are regular ferries to Cowes from here.

Sanditon

1. If, Isabella, you do not wish to be apart, hurry your steps to catch up with your friends.
2. The couple rambled through the neglected garden, hampered by brambles and nettles that caught their clothes and stung their hands.
3. It should not have been difficult for Emma to park, errors in the judgement of the width of the phaeton notwithstanding, as there was plenty of space and few other carriages in the vicinity.
4. Charlotte was keen to invite the beau for tea in order to introduce her sister Maria to a wider circle of eligible men.
5. It was difficult to find willing denizens of the forest to come out of hiding so that we could get to know them better.
6. Although on the short side, Philadelphia found the Hindi an admirable foil for her pale skin and golden tresses.
7. Elinor changed her position as the sun was glaringly bright on that side of the room.
8. The wooden seat was so rough that Frank had to sand it on both sides before applying the paint and clear varnish.
9. She ran away as fast as she could with a bank of overflow water looming threateningly behind her.
10. Mrs Elton's butler speedily went for Lot Six, the gardener bid for Lot Seven but, not so quick off the mark, for the char, Lot Ten was better than nothing.

The Watsons

1. Was it indeed, expected of her to marry a man who had a townhouse as well as one in the country?
2. Sergeant Ravenscar reviewed the new recruits with a jaundiced eye and then roared his commands, thus unnerving the squad at the outset.
3. The wretched war damage was not just a physical legacy but one that disabled many a man mentally for the rest of his life.
4. Both arms amputated at Salamanca you say, but still, he manages to earn a living sufficient to support his family?
5. Mrs John Dashwood went wild, constant on one thing only and that was a demand for more money.
6. How, at so nice a place as the Derbyshire Dales, can you possibly not enjoy the walks?
7. It was so clearly an open elopement of Lady Anne Abdy and Lord Charles Bentinck that everyone was able to guess at it and thus no secret at all.
8. Those words must calm us, grave thoughts though they may be, and so we should all pull through in the end.
9. The madcap, tainted with a questionable reputation, was no suitable match for their daughter.
10. I must tell you how ardently I admire and love you.

Volume, the First

1. You cannot rip every piece of paper into shreds that does not satisfy your high expectations.

2. There was the evidence, in just one uneven row, the mark of a shallow heel-bar, rows of footsteps in the muddy ones and plenty of other confusions wherever they searched for the poacher.

3. It was a bedraggled garden that she viewed from the window waiting for him to appear out of the depressing sheets of rain.

4. Given her hesitant good nature, Lizzy was surprised when Jane made herself rid a household of greedy relations with more grit and gut than she supposed her sister possessed.

5. At Barton Cottage, the Dashwood's had one area of red erica and another of pink but decided that it was sufficient so looked for different hardy plants for the remaining heath-like beds that weren't devoted to vegetables or herbs.

6. Richard thought carefully but, in the end, would agree not to stir an inch more than was necessary.

7. Tom Parker was fun, clever and everything a husband should be apart from his dreadful laugh which sounded like a donkey with constipation.

8. She would never consult a nasty woman like that again however difficult it was to find another expert.

9. Did it never occur, a tender minute, to your unkindness, your unrelenting sarcasm, that the child may have been telling the truth?

10. It was a choice between braving the cliff or descending by the longer route down to the beach.

1. On that basis, terrible retribution will be brought down upon your head before you know it.

2. Kitty will collect the hats; Lydia will muster lingerie and Maria will bring up the rear with all of the shawls.

3. Observing the exhibits in Mr Jones' Emporium of Exotic Displays, George noted that the basic lair, especially of the big cats, was nothing more impressive than a few shrubs and some rocks.

4. She said that it was below a lesser outcrop of rocks in Lyme Regis where Mary Anning had made her astounding discoveries of fossils.

5. If you do not direct the public up, I do not think they will tolerate seats where they cannot see John Wesley speak.

6. Mary went on and on in a droning voice, quoting liberally from Fordyce's Sermons, her long tale becomes a saga that bored the company to tears.

7. It does not matter from where she comes, she is a beloved friend who will do whatever she can to help.

8. If you total both groups of boys, I will count the number of girls in the other two groups.

9. You can't just ban quotations from Cowper as it will offend the vicar who is very partial to *The Task*.

10. Edmund agreed to counsel more people in a week than he had been undertaking in the past but protested that he would not be able to be so thorough.

1. Their relationship was platonic on certain days but when they were alone it became more intimate.
2. There will be several guests: us and, of course, the Thorpes, plus the Morlands and the Allens making ten in all to sit down to dinner.
3. Stuart will bring the drum Monday, but you may only have its loan for three days, otherwise, it incurs a penalty.
4. I assure you; Mrs Austen will be devilish ill in getting there unless we give her some laudanum or find some better form of transport.
5. It will drag the grammar lower down the scale unless we employ a better tutor for those whose achievement is not up to standard.
6. The cart will have to transport many more loads of stone if the road is to be finished by the end of the month.
7. An idea might be to employ only some of the cast least of all those who cannot remember their words.
8. I will have all of those at the back, please, plus the two in the middle as well as that pretty one at the front of the counter.
9. She was nevertheless a heroic harlot tending the poor and needy when she was both poor and needy herself.
10. The gypsies took the stolen raw rabbit meat from the bag and spread a handful on Donwell Abbey's lawn to entice the dogs away from the stables where they had an eye on a promising colt.

1. It is true that whether she is neither happy or kind, you will always be drawn to a person who smiles like that.

2. As they looked at the book together, Margaret Dashwood was assured by Edward that it was indeed a great man jousting on the beautifully caparisoned horse with plaited mane and flowing tail.

3. Jane found it difficult to pamper kinship when she disliked her Aunt Austen-Leigh so much.

4. Cassandra and Jane were gathered together at the spa in the centre of Cheltenham for their health, but it was also a good opportunity to socialise.

5. Miss Carteret was bedecked in jewellery including a circlet upon her head, and on her arm, a dazzling array of bracelets, not to mention the rings on nearly every finger.

6. To ensure that her family understood why she would marry Lieutenant Price, Frances Ward decided that less explanation would be a better strategy.

7. Nothing will ever hamper cynicism when such a worldly-wise person gives vent to her feelings.

8. Charlotte Collins was such a happy mother as she watched her children collecting daisies to make into a chain.

9. The costume was not to her liking, so Harriet fiddled with the pompom, fretting all the while and wishing that she had chosen to be something other than Harlequins' Columbina.

10. Kitty stared at the gentleman and wondered if some show-off other—in gay abandon—would make a fool of himself in such company.

Lady Susan

1. They were very thankful that the cat had her kittens in the barn rather than in the kitchen.
2. It was a dreadfully inhuman war in gigantic proportions though the dictator denied it.
3. If you think of humanism, it has a certain ring of hopefulness.
4. Although it was touch and go, Henry did, with the aid of the Regent's surgeon and Jane's dedicated nursing, recover nonetheless, for which mercy everyone was relieved
5. The maid was deceitful over and over again and, in the end, they had to turn her out of the house without a reference.
6. Cubism art in the early twentieth century was a revolutionary approach to representing reality.
7. Naming them Teepee and Pigwig more or less spoke volumes for the inventive imagination with which the child named her toys.
8. Lydia thought it a fantastic lark, especially as it did no one any harm and provided her with a great deal of fun and laughter.
9. On top of Mount Ararat, a damp ark lands and Noah with his sons—Ham, Seth and Japheth—looks out and espies the rainbow.

10. The flowers were mostly sent from admirers and a few came from other friends in Meryton.

Plan of a Novel

1. Whenever she was present, I mentioned his name, knowing very well that it annoyed her immensely.
2. The Parson travelled as far north as to Berwick, educating the poor and unfortunate in every village where he stopped.
3. Marianne was too hasty leaving the company in distress so nobody knew where she was going or how long she would be or whether she would return at all.
4. It was a sticking point and Anna valiantly kept to her own opinion even though her stepmother was most unhappy about the whole situation.
5. It was a comic rave Neddy acted out in the Austen theatricals performed in their barn that winter.
6. Yesterday it was the Iambic our tourist guide took us to and we found these columns much more to our liking, striking a balance between the Corinthian which were too fanciful or the Doric which were too plain.
7. Lizzy was practising her French but when it came out as the "Roi ne pas" she thought perhaps that she hadn't got it quite right when Georgiana gave a little giggle.
8. It was a risky business to up the anti the same way that he had done in the past.

9. Some thought that it was nevertheless wrong if, for different reasons, Wickham went about charming the newest heiress to arrive in the town.

10. To be frank, nigh ten times as many sheep would not compensate for the loss Sir Thomas sustained in the snowstorm.

Letters I

1. It was Wickham's loan even though he denied ever knowing anything about it.

2. There was no hope, not in a month of Sundays, of ever having the debt repaid.

3. There was no sign at urethra exits, nor in the whole of the canal, that the disease was being harboured by Mr Knightley's cows and he was relieved that he would not have to have them destroyed.

4. Edward Knight was worried that there appeared to be widespread and prolific harm out Hampshire way although it seemed to be under control now.

5. Colonel Brandon did not want any reward in cash, but if the Dashwoods wished they may send him something in kind.

6. Elinor was only measuring the distance from the door to the window so that she knew how large a carpet the room could accommodate.

7. The meetings were non-stop, ostensibly to cater for those students who came newly to the university and needed something to give them confidence.

8. He was stymied at every turning and became so frustrated that he let out an almighty scream as he pounded the door with his clenched fist.

9. My own beloved earth, how I extol thee and how I bless thee for producing such wonderful potatoes.

10. Miss Bates is terribly upset you know and there is nothing that we can do to make it any better for her.

Letters II

1. "You can take an economy seat on the stage, Miss Morland, and be home without any trouble at all," said General Tilney with a withering effect.

2. Isabella grabbed the cameo, gleefully running away from James and hiding behind a shrub to study his silhouette before he could snatch it back from her.

3. Young Ladies such as Miss Lydia Black all the accomplishments necessary for an eligible marriage.

4. In the shop window, yards upon yards of muslin, tulle and other delectable material hung in a beautiful, beguiling rainbow of promise.

5. The Dashwoods decided to grow ling-simply because it would be the only plant capable of surviving in that bleak spot in their garden.

6. The plump, trembling hand of Lady Dalrymple grasped her binoculars, holding them up to peruse the company and thus dismissing her upstart Elliot relations.

7. Looking at the two green sprigs in her hand, Elinor wondered if she should add the woman's herb or nettle to the brew to make it more palatable.

8. With cunning Willoughby took her to the window where he showed an appreciation of landscaped art (for devious reasons known only to himself) and, combined with charm, he completely deceived the innocent girl with whom he had questionable designs.

9. Mrs Bennet and her two youngest daughters were driven over to Netherfield, ostensibly to be assured of the welfare of Jane but they all had their own hidden agenda.

10. Emma blissfully assumed that she was adequately adept for drawing the likeness of Harriet to please Mr Elton.

Textual Strategies

1. Oh, *mon ami*, a bleeding heart is a sorrowful state but tomorrow the sun will surely shine for you.

2. "I am most disappointed," said Mrs Norris. "I lent the book to you, Fanny, thinking it would improve your secretive ways."

3. With the threat of doom, Ann erred on the side of caution to prevent any such thing happening.

4. Darcy was furious with the servant as tempers were not tolerated at Pemberley.

5. Of a good crop of ripe strawberries Mr Knightley was sure, as on every day for the past month the sun had shone warmly and the rain had fallen lightly.

6. John Thorpe was stuck in the first rut, his hands on the reins, pulling quite in the wrong direction with too much force and the horses were almost out of control.

7. Whatever the cook made, served on a suitable platter, it was always appreciated by the company.

8. Eleanor, dressed in white, a la mode, stood in the doorway in all her elegance, causing a pause in the conversation.

9. "Well, Bella, I'm able to find plenty of excuses to oblige Miss Morland, but I'm d****d if I'll do the same for you, my dear sister."

10. Mrs Hill thought that the cake would look smart if iced delicately with a pink rose and green marchpane leaves to set it off.

Publication

1. If eating brown bread is not working, then rye is maybe the answer or perhaps a loaf that is seeded might help.

2. There was the evocative perfume of cedar lingering in her bedroom that took me back to my childhood and the soap that Nanny used in my bath.

3. You are, gentlemen, the very epitome of what is best about England and I am proud to call you my friends.

4. I did beg 'er to not go oop that thar path yer H'onner but she would do so and with that thar 'evvy bag a dragging of be'ind 'er, she was sure ter come ter grief yer H'onner, Sir Thomas, sir.

5. The Gardiner's daughter had either combed it or done something different to the doll's hair making it look newer than it actually was.

6. George Austen and James, his son, inspected every pew, termites having infested some of the rafters and

they worried that the creatures might find their way into all of the woodwork in the church.

7. The stream was just a murmur, rays of a gentle sun blessing the ripples with a sparkling light that completed the idyllic scene enjoyed by Marianne and Willoughby.

8. Frank gritted his teeth as he made the climb, rocking the branches as he went from one to another in an effort to rescue the stranded cat.

9. Don't fret Tristan, I erased that mistake long before anyone could take offence.

10. Elinor searched the rolls of cloth, but she could find no velvet the colour to match or complement the gown that Marianne would be wearing for the coming ball.

Pewter

1. Once again, her itinerary included Chawton, Alton, Andover and Winchester.

2. Whatever the charade, James was able to cap it always with a better one of his own.

3. Fakes were easily detected in his Cubism works but in his Art Deco no microscopic inspection ever exposed his forgeries.

4. It may work with a G-clef or tune it to a better in C.

5. Hear no evil, see no evil, speak no evil.

6. The stagecoach took Henry to a cold and blustery Oban, keeping him from alighting and thus he continued his journey into the heart of Scotland without even stepping into an inn for a mulled wine.

7. Jane could not understand how age should determine whether or not she was ready to be sent away to school.

8. Lack of fortune would not curb us in essentials but there would be no money for the elegancies of life.

9. The horse was clumsy in negotiating the steep bank, rupturing its spleen, breaking a foreleg and thus ending all hope for a promising mount for the Vine hunt.

10. Mr Woodhouse would be laid in his coffin come the winter and the Knightley's would establish themselves in Donwell before the spring.

Literature

1. It was not an easy task, but Harriet shooed off Mr Martin's cow, permitting the child to pass through the gate without too much of a problem.

2. Without thought, he threw off his nightgown and pulled the long johns on before reaching for his trousers and shirt.

3. "Don't worry Marianne," said Colonel Brandon, "the grand is on its way and will be in the salon in time for tuning before our guests arrive."

4. The Gardiner children went chasing around the room screaming as the soap bubbles gave a delightful pop every time one burst and showered them with droplets of soapy water

5. The cat entered the room with sleek negligence then jumped onto the baby's cot to sleep in peace for the rest of the afternoon.

6. Harry was spoiled dreadfully and, with a little trot, ran to Mrs Palmer to complain about the lack of attention he was receiving.

7. "You should put a clean halter on the horse Maria if you are to impress the Rushworths," said Tom.

8. In the temple, they came across a tub-urn such as was found in the ancient society who had lived in the valley below.

9. Whilst they stayed at the camp, bells rang out to call them to a meal but on the march, it was the drums that kept them in order.

10. Mary was charmed by rondos and wondered if her tutor could introduce her to Mozart's Rondo a la Turk which was a very fast one.

Landmark Advances

1. As Charles Bingley looked down at his baby son, dangling his fob, rocking the cradle and crooning a lullaby, he was the proudest father in the whole of Staffordshire.

2. He runs, he shouts out, "Hampson, come back, all is well," but the man does not listen and is soon out of sight.

3. Catharine tended to call an eagle a bird of prey but, after Henry's gentle encouragement, in future she called it a raptor—rather like his father, she thought.

4. Darcy walked Lizzy by the Pemberley stream and crossed where it divided into a sweet rill in green pastures and where it gave a romantic touch to the whole scene.

5. It was a strenuous climb up but at midday they had reached the summit, to Nancy's relief, and they would almost certainly be back at the lodge in time for tea.

6. Ann thought that she saw a phantom, a lingering likeness of the man she still loved.

7. The coffee house was a central hub, back in the eighteenth century, for meetings of men with like minds.

8. Lizzy thought it odd that a young lady such as her friend Charlotte Lucas should consider marrying the buffoon, Mr Collins.

9. It was not possible to undo Odysseus' rather scruffy likeness from Emma's efforts to embroider slippers for Mr Knightley but perhaps he would not notice.

10. It was just a little tipple Fay enjoyed that evening before retiring to bed, but she resolved that she would not imbibe again.

Controversy

1. Catherine escaped to a secret arbor in great haste to avoid meeting with the rather amorous soldier.

2. He sat on the summit for days, his food supplies dwindling at an alarming rate until he was eventually rescued.

3. The housekeeper was making sandwiches for the picnic and kept in mind that ham is Emma's favourite filling.

4. In that particular sitcom, men tended to be the better at delivering the jokes.

5. He was a landlord in Aryan appearance and Aryan behaviour and was the most popular Aryan host in the town.
6. On the Brecon, tents tended to be buffeted alarmingly and could be blown away if not securely pegged.
7. With aplomb, Ron tended the girl's ankle, believing it to be a pretence to gain his attention.
8. Mr Collins took too much sugar so no wonder his teeth were deteriorating at an alarming rate.
9. When James arrived, he called in for a quick 'hello' at Henry's stables to check on the horse before walking up the hill to find the man himself.
10. Edward's attempt at reading Cowper turned out to be a badly read verse even in Elinor's opinion.

The Church

1. If Catherine did not stand erect or at least give him her complete attention, General Tilney was dismissive of her questions.
2. Captain Wentworth looked up as torrid waters fell fast and furiously down the inside of the ship and into the bilge below.
3. The Reverend Samuel Cooke looked on, astounded that such urchins should be so ungrateful at his generous gesture.
4. Catherine applied herself to the embroidery as the never ever ending task threatened to spoil an afternoon of cricket with her brothers.
5. Maurice was the biggest loser Monty had ever met.

6. The whole strategy will gel tonight and thus our future ensured.
7. It was an almost dead bluetit Henry rescued from the jaws of the cat and he hoped that Jane would work her magic on the pathetic bird.
8. Singing did not occur at every service, but it was always a pleasure when it did.
9. The farm labourers tossed the hay, terrifying any animal that may have been trapped there, much to the enjoyment of the men and sport for the dogs.
10. What if Isabella is left behind and can't find her way home?

War, Politics and Religion

1. Mr Wickham's drinking habit was a concern, but he always promised that he would stop it tomorrow.
2. The clever pun restored his reputation as a man of discerning grammar.
3. Southcliff ran central to the strategy and they were confident of success.
4. First Patrick and then Ryan argued the Irish corner and very nearly won the day.
5. The Reverend George Austen roped uprights together and then a pole on the top of the structure completed it so that a sheet could be draped across and make a splendid tent in which his children may shelter and play.
6. There was a big swarm yesterday, but Sir William East located the Queen bee and removed her and the

swarm from the apple tree before transferring them into his vacant hive.
7. The use of the Italian Enrico operating as a stagehand as well as a tenor saved the show.
8. The red-hot axe severed the bull's head in one fell swoop of the slaughterer's two arms.
9. The monk from Cardiff ran Cistercian monasteries with an efficiency to be admired by any who came to enquire.
10. When I took the children to the menagerie and the cause of a commotion appeared to be a camel, I zapped it with a blow to its behind, threw a blanket over its head and it dropped to its knees.

Dress

1. He realised that acquiring ownership did not necessarily mean that he had control.
2. There was nothing for it but to make the best of a bad job, but Tom Parker would go away with at least his pride intact.
3. It must not become a whim, us lingering in this way, but perhaps a more definite approach would bring a positive result.
4. The Gardiner children were blowing bubbles again and the sound of a gentle pop linked the present with Jane's memory from long ago.
5. Selina was adamant that she could spot tedious people as soon as they walked into the room and would steer her friend into more lively company.

6. Martha wiped the jam pot rim, mingling soap in warm water to ensure that a clean jar was in readiness for the blackberry jam when it had boiled for a sufficient length of time

7. Discovering the hub on networking the organisation of the protesting millworkers, he thought perhaps he had solved the mystery of their success.

8. A plate of tasty rib bones accompanied the thick steaming soup and a newly baked cottage loaf, helped down with a tankard of ale, set Sidney up for a pleasant evening.

9. If you think that I am bereft of all indifference then you have sadly misunderstood my feelings.

10. It was indeed a muntjac on eternal wonderings though the Rushworth's estate causing untold damage as it munched and meandered its way from one boundary to another and even the ha-ha didn't stop it.

Accomplishments and Virtues

1. Robert poured the brandy shots in gin glasses and hoped that no one would complain.

2. Anne was forced to withdraw in gathering alarm, wondering where on earth she could retreat to next without being discovered in her agitation at the appearance of Frederick Wentworth in the salon.

3. She knew that it didn't matter which arm was presented, the cowpox injection urged upon her by Mrs Lefroy, was going to hurt.

4. Maria enjoyed all of the running races even though she often came last.

5. Eleanor was an acknowledged connoisseur of furnishings and had spoken about décor umpteen times but the last was always as fresh as the first.

6. The Radical stood on his soapbox speaking in a convincing rhetoric and it was a pure ad in getting them to listen and learn for future enlightenment.

7. Edward took his son George to the lathe although he was still rather young and small to be able to work it by himself.

8. We had to tackle this wearying marathon ourselves, but it was with a great sense of achievement when every article of clothing that we had made was sold and our coffers once more fit to support us.

9. To begin with, the rewards will be small, but you will, in the next phase, win great accolades.

10. It was Christmas and so Sally and I joined the choir to hum our background accompaniment to their sopranos, contraltos and tenors.

Pastimes and Entertainment

1. Mary's performance on the pianoforte would be improved, she thought, with arpeggios, accelerator and allegretto—but the audience were of a different opinion.

2. Francis ran to the Hythe at recession and returned just in time for the last lecture of the day.

3. The apothecary was able to throw alkaline substances into the pot to activate a reasonable result.

4. I fell in the pigsty, so I reeked of manure when I shook hands with the man.

5. Lady Hester Stanhope discovered that it was semi-arid in greater parts of the dessert but further south it was mostly sand.

6. Young John Knight was anxious to show his two pennies at the Highbury baker's and wondered how many sugared buns he could buy with that small fortune.

7. It was the bebop era of jazz in those days and musically it was a very exciting time despite the restrictions of the war.

8. It certainly looked authentic on certificates that were handwritten before the invention of the typewriter.

9. The great man showed no tact organising such an opulent display in front of the Prince Regent.

10. Mrs Norris was put out at tin guards instead of the usual iron mesh and was in no doubt that they would be useless.

Children

1. We are fortunate to live in town because it gives us an advantage when shopping for almost everything.

2. Because the captain grew ill, I amputated his foot as it had become gangrenous and would have caused his death.

3. As to regard in errors of etiquette, the two younger Bennet girls were forever committing them much to Jane and Lizzy's chagrin.

4. For Cassandra to wait for the carriage would mean narrowly missing an opportunity to meet with her

niece so she walked the short distance between the two houses.

5. If Henry did not steady the fulcrum or land a fish with his hand-held rod there would be no dinner tonight.
6. Mark me well, I otherwise may refuse to endorse your application as tutor to Sir John's sons.
7. "I am not sure your pal merits such devotion Henry," said his father, "because every time you are together you end up in trouble."
8. Just because Miss Bates may be a bit eccentric, hardly anyone took notice of her funny little ways.
9. It was all your fault, Lydia.
10. Catherine was uncertain whether to put the injured bird in a cage or get a box that would be warmer and she could always pierce the lid to allow it to breathe.

Status

1. Be sure that it will occur at every corner of Mansfield Park until proper measures are put into place.
2. Catherine's brother George Morland was only a lad, yet his achievements were quite incredible.
3. Henry jumped over the bar onto the grass beyond and then raced to the road for help.
4. Marco, lonely and listless, put his head in his hands and prayed that someone would come to his rescue.
5. It was a good idea to briefly stop, reach Ermine Street and then take his bearings from there.
6. Edwards Knight's plan was to endow age-related persons with a pension appropriate to their status and length of service.

7. Charlotte had to pull or drag the box over to her grandmother so that she could inspect the contents.

8. It was a smidgen era, literally a small, unimportant one that was sandwiched between two great geological ages.

9. Bring thine petty fiasco unto mine own house to receive my forgiving blessing for erring and go thy way in peace to make good thine mistakes.

10. "The Rev, Angel, is true to his calling," said the disrespectful Mary Crawford to her closest friend, "and his is the last profession into which I would marry."

Position in Society

1. Mary took the food into the dining room and then took the dirty dishes out to the kitchen.

2. "Take the clock to the window where you can see Betsy," said Mrs Austen "and rewind it, but not too tight on that spring."

3. The gold was to be found on the bottom of a pebble and sand riverbed, but it took a long and tedious time to sort it from the gravel.

4. It was Charles who gave Cassandra and Jane the oval etchings and Francis was the source of the amber necklaces.

5. The top of the hill brought the regiment to a wiser vantage point than lower down where they would not have been able to see the enemy.

6. Sarah opened a market stall as there was an upsurge on the sales of wool and embroidery thread.

7. "Discard the weaklings, Mr Collins," advised Lady de Bourgh, "but cherish those who show promise."
8. "I do love to add jam, especially when it is spread on a scone before adding clotted cream and a fresh strawberry," declared Mrs Elton.
9. "Oh, Ma I didn't do it," he said, "and please don't' blame me for the pig escaping either."
10. Take your horse to the mart in Tattersalls because that is where the best deals are to be found.

Food and Drink

1. "Nuts, any nuts," Mrs Elton complained, "even if I eat just one single chestnut, megrim will surely follow and keep me in bed for days on end."
2. Whatever you need or have, get a blessed grasp on your bearings before setting out as I don't want a message to say that you are without some essential or other.
3. Thorpe was determined to win, stuffing his mouth with as much as he could manage which was a test early on in the competition to see who could eat the most meat pies.
4. It was dark above the stairs but there seemed to be no threat and Mr Tilney had gone to Woodston, so up Catherine went albeit rather nervously.
5. Mrs Bennet had not believed in nervous complaints of others but was profuse in declaring her own.
6. It is all very well to make things difficult but termly tests is taking it a bit too far.

7. Little Harry was not averse to a thump or kick and thought a pinch now and then would gain attention.

8. The farmer with his wagon is a kindly soul and thus usually picks up persons who are walking to market and takes not a penny for his troubles.

9. Francis pulled hard on the oars in an effort to get to a stable mooring on the River Itchen where he could tie up his boat for the night.

10. Catherine went below in evermore hesitating steps, worried what she would find in the cellar.

Medical

1. It was perfectly alright to conjoin valid situations providing they did not interfere with the general run of things.

2. Caroline Bingley was determined to equip ill-serving members with permission-to-leave cards as soon as possible.

3. Robert admitted that it is impossible to grasp rainbows and there certainly isn't a pot of gold at the end.

4. My dear, you must wear it if it suits you but don't blame me if it turns out to be wrong for the occasion.

5. Take it from me, the Pontiff ain't in gorgeous robes because he is showing off but because they are the traditional garb of his station.

6. The gang make their way along the narrow path as the guides urge on the need to make haste which does not threaten their safety in any way.

7. It wasn't everyone's idea to nick the old hag's book but certainly, most of the class thought it would be fun to hide it from her.

8. The nettles stung Lizzy's ankle, so she found the leaf of a doc to reduce the uncomfortable, stinging itch where great white bumps were appearing.

9. It was imperative that they flee, chasing the departing chaise that might leave without their rescue.

10. The young gentleman's idea was to press, woo, nurture then declare his love for the beautiful daughter of Lord Mansfield.

Buildings

1. She realised in the end that even if she ran a faster race, she would never beat her rival to the winning posts.

2. "Ma'am," said he in a superior voice, "if lobster is beyond your purse, then let a crab be your choice," and the poor woman turned her head in embarrassment.

3. Kitty and Lydia giggled their way to Meryton, determined to find a handsome man or in any event, a man who was not bad looking with whom to flirt and dance.

4. The echo velocity of the yodelling in the valley was beyond any sound experienced by Edward Knight on his Grand Tour.

5. Susan found the children and then took them home with all the berries and scratches that they had collected.

6. Directing the servants, Mrs Norris told them, "After inspecting the wainscot, tag every piece of furniture that is to be removed from this room."

7. Miss Bates was bandaged from toes to ankle after she had carelessly picked up a hot, elderly saucepan and dropped it onto her foot when the handle finally parted company.

8. Henry was keen to be introduced to the girl as soon as she entered the room and was in nervous anticipation as the means soon presented itself.

9. In my young days, the choice was hopscotch, skipping or spinning a top, none of these silly rhymes whilst clapping hands or touching toes.

10. Marianne was despondent and cast leaf after leaf into the stream watching them float away, just like the dreams that she now realised would come to nothing.

The Picturesque and Landscape Gardening

1. Marianne's psyche was manic, raw for days on end, and no one but Elinor could soothe or help her through the days and nights.

2. It was the fourth arc our triumphant forbears declared the best decorated of the six that formed the bridge over the river.

3. Not quite a Nabob, Rowntree was nevertheless a tremendous contributor to the welfare of his people and the community in general.

4. "It is Sarah! Aha, we have caught you in the act you thieving little beggar," exclaimed Thorpe as he grabbed her ear and dragged her out of the pantry.

5. It is thus, so the R to number 6 in S row keeps the Robinsons away from the Steeles.
6. Only one more item, please, as we must not overload the donkey cart.
7. Slowly the cat advanced and crept on ever closer to her prey, paused and then pounced.
8. There is no use taking old Smith at his word for he is most unreliable.
9. She was histrionic at her inexperience in the matter and therefore her judgement was in question.
10. Sally must read lest Roper gets ideas about his sister taking over the task of entertaining Lady Dalrymple.

Transport and Travel

1. He drove the donkey from Ravenscar to the countryside trusting that the parcels were securely tied to the panniers.
2. It was unnecessary to throw such an obvious, less than subtle quip agents were sure to dislike and thus lessen the possibility of being chosen.
3. Henry Tilney selected the venue carefully as he wanted it to be a special treat for their honeymoon.
4. They would condemn her anyway whether it was for being a witch or several counts of treachery.
5. Returning from India and using the vernacular, Philadelphia and Eliza declared that a cup of cha is every bit a drink to be savoured as any other beverage in England.
6. Now, wouldn't that be an achievement—to land a unicorn or catch a griffin?

7. It was a matter of choice whether he would jump ostensibly into the fray or stand back and let others do so.

8. Not just a gentleman, my dear, but a rich gentleman to boot so make sure that you dress appropriately and mind your manners.

9. If it wasn't a tele-phantom for their next theatricals, then it was something queer going on in the barn like a villager playing the fool.

10. To give Denny and co a chance to make good their mistake was probably the best way forward.

The Thames Valley

1. The sassy kestrel hovered above its prey, at an unbelievable height, before swooping down upon the unfortunate animal below.

2. The Sharps denied all knowledge of the people and declared that they had never visited anywhere near where they lived.

3. If we go to war, grave outcomes are inevitable.

4. It was a surprise to the Highbury residents when ley-lines crossed two sides of their village.

5. Trevithick's car let several daring people experience a ride in it as it was towed by his noisy iron engine along a Cornish street.

6. Charles bent down to scoop Ermintrude the escapist chicken up into his arms and quickly dispatched the hen by wringing her neck.

7. In their old age, Mr and Mrs George Austen could recall eight children who, like every family, had brought them worries but mostly joys and pride.

8. Thorpe would eat any bread in greedy haste, especially if it was spread with a generous helping of dripping.

9. He yelled loudly with the intention to spur le Yacine on to a greater victory in the field of combat.

10. For goodness' sake don't let that ham espy me in the audience because he is sure to overact the mimic.

Oxford

1. Mr Knightley collected the jewellery box for delivering to Emma as soon as he returned from London.

2. Mr Yates hoped to give a sterling performance in their theatricals, but he was caught out by Sir Thomas.

3. The sting of the wasp racked Charlotte's hand for days on end and not even Mr Collins' remedy could ease the pain.

4. The Bennets ended up with twenty pots of jam, especially of blackberry, which accounted for almost half of them.

5. The cricket team will include Theo, Phil, Usama, Kaan and Edward for certain but we still have at least six more members to contact.

6. Mrs Phillips always shopped at the Co-op, ergo a welcome bonus to spend at Christmas.

7. These boxes hold twenty-four examples and are especially designed to be safely transported so phials with the serum must be packed in them and then put into cold storage until collected.

8. "The so-called war department has let us down once again Darcy," Colonel Forster complained, "and I find that the Regiment must remove from Brighton and head to the east coast."

9. Deciding upon a suitable profession for his sons was important to Mr Austen and having sent Frank into the Royal Navy, and with that success Charles entered that service also.

10. Sir John Middleton put his horse to stud entirely against the advice of Colonel Brandon.

Bath

1. Mrs Bennet had invited Bingley and Darcy to supper, rotating the seating arrangements from one plan to another before finally settling on the one that placed Darcy furthest away from herself.

2. Jane walked away disappointedly, measuring her steps in a slow retreat from a fruitless visit to the Bingley town residence.

3. The child put a thumb at her mouth, but seeing the disapproving look from her mother, quickly took it away to show that she was not going to suck it.

4. He was neither a judge or germane to the enquiry so Mr Bennet allowed Darcy to deal with the matter as he thought fit.

5. Darcy often went for a ride at his aunt's manor so Lizzy should not have been surprised to see him trotting towards her.
6. The past event on everyone's mind was not one of mutual happiness.
7. The residents at Newal Cottage were a pleasant family whom everyone liked.
8. When Sir Thomas Bertram's chef introduced couscous into the menu it was under the mistaken belief that his master had enjoyed it in Antigua.
9. Her near faint caused him to give her a barbaric lift only out of sheer frustration rather than unkindness.
10. It was fair weather when she left the house but now Marianne was out in gusty wind and the threat of rain.

London

1. The worsening of the weather encouraged Lucy's urge onwards towards home at a quickening pace.
2. The child was very distressed until songs sung by Nanny soothed her and gradually the crying ceased.
3. Although the situation was chronic, it yet had some benefit in the growing confidence of the man as he overcame his adversity.
4. In their tour of Cornwall, Henry drove her in his carriage all the way to The Lizard and back to Truro for dinner.
5. Lady Lucas did not hold with air balloons and thought Lizzy too daring for words when she heard that she had ascended in one even though it was safely tethered.

6. When I saw them, I greeted them enthusiastically much to everyone's delight.

7. As the room was so hot Elizabeth dampened down the fire and opened the windows, much to Mrs Bennet's annoyance.

8. What heat remained was sufficient to keep them comfortably warm until it was time for tea.

9. Whoever you call on, do not outstay your welcome, my dear, for it is bad manners for a young lady to do so for longer than twenty minutes.

10. In Bath, both ostlers and stable hands prided themselves on their speed and efficiency when the Stage or Post drew up to the inn.

Recommended Reading and Viewing

NB All books quoted are from my own shelves. Other publications can be sought by Googling.

Jane Austen a Family Life...............*Jane Austen A Life* Clair Tomlin 1997 Viking

Sense and Sensibility........... *Jane Austen's Regency Dashwoods* Alan Firth 2019 Grosvenor House Pub

Pride and Prejudice ....*The Cambridge Companions to Jane Austen* ed Copeland and McMaster2014

DVD *Bride and Prejudice* A Gurinda Chadha Film

Mansfield Park ....*Belle* Paula Byrne William Collins 2014

Lovers Vows Mrs Inchbald Jefferson Publication 2015

Emma .... *Jane Austen Collected Poems and Verses* ed David Selwyn 1996

The Highbury Trilogy Allie Cresswell 2018 Amazon

DVD *Clueless* starring Alicia Silverstone

Persuasion ....*Jane Austen and the Navy* Brian Southam 2005 National Maritime Museum

Northanger Abbey ....f..*A Gossip's Story* Jane West (Vallencourt books)

Sanditon ....*Jane Austen's Sanditon* ed
Kathryn Sutherland 2016 Oxford World Classics

The Watsons .... *The Younger Sister* Mrs
Hubback (Amazon)

Volume the First .... *The Rivals* Richard Brinsley
Sheridan

Love and Freindship – Volume the Second .... *Volume the Second* intro Kathryn Sutherland 2014 Abbeville Press
Publishers

Lesley Castle—also from Volume the Second........ ditto and
Vol the First and Vol the Third

The History of England ....*The History of England* ed
Deidre Le Faye (Facsimile) The British Library

Lady Susan ....DVD *Love and Freindship*
Lionsgate – Curzon

Plan of a Novel .... *Jane Austen Minor Works*
ed R W Chapman 1954 Oxford University Press

Letters I ....*Jane Austen's Letters* 3rd
edition. Deidre Le Faye 1995 Oxford University Press

Letters II.................. ditto ... .

Textual Strategies ....*Some Words of Jane Austen*
Stuart M Tave 1973 University of Chicago Press

Publication .... *Jane's Fame* Claire Harman
2009 Canongate Books Ltd

Jane Austen Cover to Cover 2014 Quirk Productions Inc

Pewter .... *Jane Austen the Banker's Sister* E
J Clery 2017 Biteback Publishers Ltd

Literature ....*The Task and Other Poems* William
Cowper printed by Amazon

Landmark Advances ....*The Jane Austen Files*
Helen Amy 2015 Amberley Publishing

Controversy .... gp *The Janeite's Dream Book of Trivia* Bascom and Wallis (Amazon)

f *Debits and Credits* Rudyard Kipling 1926 Macmillan

The Church ....*Jane Austen and the Clergy* Irene Collins 1994 The Hambledon Press

Praying With Jane Rachel Dodge 2018 Bethany House

War, Politics and Religion ....*Jane Austen and the French Revolution* Warren Roberts 1995 The Athlone Press

Jane Austen—Writing Social, Politics Tom Keymar 2020 Oxford University Press

Dress ....gp *Dress-up Jane Austen* Bruzzone and Haworth 2017 www.bsmall,co.uk

Google 17th and 18th Century Rural Artists

Accomplishments and Virtues ....*Jane Austen's Sewing Box* Jennifer Forest 2009 Murdoch Books

Pastimes and Entertainment .... *A Dance with Jane Austen* Susannah Fullerton 2012 Frances Lincoln Ltd

Jane Austen and Leisure David Selwyn 1999 The Hambledon Press

Children..................... *Jane Austen and Children*, David Selwyn 2010 Continuum

Status .... *Georgette Heyer's Regency World* Jennifer Kloester 2005 Arrow Books

Position in Society ....f *Longbourn* Jo Baker 2013 Black Swan

f Any book by Georgette Heyer

Food and Drink ....*Jane Austen's Country Life* Deidre Le Faye 2014 Frances Lincoln Ltd

sp *The Jane Austen Diet* Bryan Kozlowski 2019 pub Turner

Medical ....any book concerning Edward Jenner and Smallpox

Buildings ....*Jane and Me, My Austen Heritage*
Caroline Jane Knight 2017 The Graham Group
The Picturesque and Landscape Gardening ...... *Capability Brown* Shire Publications
Humphry Repton Shire Publications
Transport and Travel .... *The Great Bath Road* Daphne Phillips 1988 Countryside Books
An American in Regency England Louis Simond ed Christopher Hibbert The History Book club 1968
The Thames Valley ....*The Stranger in Reading* John May 2005 Two Rivers Press
Passages from the Diaries of Mrs Philip Lybbe Powys Ed Emily Climenson
1899 www.ForgottenBooks.Org
Oxford ....*The Curious Case of the Schoolboy who was Killed* Martin J Cowthorne 2017 Matador
Bath.....................*A Charming Place*, Maggie Lane 1988 Millstream Books
f *Lady of Quality* Georgette Heyer
London ....*Walking Jane Austen's London* Louise Allen 2013 Shire Publications
f *Frederica* Georgette Heyer

Biographical Index

Abdy,	Lady and Lord Charles Bentwick – a real-life story.
Alfred Cops	real-life manager of Tower of London menagerie
Allen, Mrs	(NA) family friend who took Catherine Morland to Bath
Anna Austen	Jane's niece
Anne, Elliot	(P) protagonist
Austen, Mrs	nee Cassandra Leigh, Jane's mother
Bates, Miss	(E) delightful chatterbox supporting character
Bennet, Mrs	(P & P) Lizzy's (Elizabeth's) mother
Bertram, Sir Thomas	(MP) owner of Mansfield Park. Fanny's uncle
Betsy	servant at Chawton Cottage
Brandon, Colonel	(S & S) supporting character, secondary love interest
Caroline, Bingley	(P & P) unpleasant sister to Charles, Mr Darcy's friend
Carteret, Miss	(P) Lady Dalrymple's relation
Cassandra Austen	Jane's beloved sister
	Jane's mother nee Leigh

Catherine Morland	(NA) Heroine
Charles Austen	Jane's naval brother
Bingley	(P & P) Mr Darcy's friend
Charlotte Lucas	(P & P) Lizzy's friend
Cowper, William	English poet 1731-1800
Dalrymple, Dowager Lady	(P) distant relation of the Elliots
Darcy, Mr Fitzwilliam	(P&P) protagonist love interest; wears a wet shirt on screen
Dashwood family	(S & S) Mrs Dashwood's un-likeable in-laws.
David	my invention
Denny	(P & P) member of the militia stationed in Meryton
Edmund Bertram	(MP) protagonist, son of Sir Thomas, Fanny's cousin
Edward Austen-Knight	Jane's rich brother also known as Neddy
Ferrars	(S & S) protagonist romantic interest
Eleanor Tilney	(NA) hero Henry's sister
Elinor Dashwood	(S & S) oldest sister, protagonist
Eliza Hancock,	Feuillide, Austen—Jane's cousin.
Eliza Austen-Knight	Jane Austen's niece
Elizabeth	(P & P) see Lizzy
Elton, Mr, the Rev	(E) newly arrived vicar of Highbury

Mrs	(E) boastful wife of the Reverend
Emma Woodhouse	(E) eponymous protagonist
Enrico	my invention
Fanny Price	(MP) protagonist, cousin to the Bertrams
Fay	my invention
Fordyce, James	1720 – 1796 pub Fordyce's Sermons 1766
Forster, Colonel	(P & P) in command of Militia based in Meryton and Brighton
Francis Austen	also known as Frank, Jane's naval brother
Frederick Wentworth	(P) sailor, protagonist romantic interest
Gardiner family	(P & P) very nice relations of the Bennets
George, Rev Austen	Jane's father
Austen	Jane's unfortunate brother
Austen-Knight	Ittle Dordy. Jane's nephew George
Knightley	(E) a gentleman protagonist
Morland	(NA) Catherine's brother
Georgiana Darcy	(P & P) Mr Darcy's sister
Goddard, Mrs	(E) runs the local girls' school in Highbury
Hampson	Rev George Austen's ancestor
Harriet	(E) orphan befriended and organised by Emma

Harry	(S & S) horrid, spoiled son of the Palmers
Hill, Mrs	(P & P) the Bennet's housekeeper
Henry Austen	Jane's banker brother
Tilney	(NA) Hero
Isabella Thorpe	(NA) Catherine Morland's one-time friend. Aka Bella
James Austen	Jane's eldest brother
Morland	(NA) Catherine's eldest brother
Jane Austen	author
Jane Bennet	(P & P) Lizzy's best sister
John Knightly	(E) Mr George Knightley's brother
	(E) Mr Knightley's nephew
Thorpe	(NA) James Morland's university friend.
Jones, Mr	my invention
Kitty Bennet	(P & P) Lizzy's sister
Knightley, Mr	(E) George. Gentleman protagonist
Lady de Bourgh	(P & P) harridan aunt of Mr Darcy
Lefroy, Mrs	Jane Austen's friend
Leigh-Perrot	Mrs Jane, sharp-tongued aunt of Jane Austen
Lizzy Bennet	(P & P) feisty protagonist. See Elizabeth
Lucas, Lady	(P & P) mother of Lizzy's friend Charlotte

Lucy Steele	(S &S) Elinor Dashwood's rival
Lydia Bennet	(P & P) Lizzy's naughty youngest sister
Mansfield, Lord	18th Century Lawyer famous for his ruling on slaves
Marco	my invention
Margaret Dashwood	(S & S) youngest sister
Maria Bertram	(MP) Fanny's cousin
Lucas	(P & P) sister of Lizzy's friend Charlotte
Marianne Dashwood	(S & S) Elinor's romantic sister. Protagonist
Martha Lloyd	companion to the Austen ladies. Married Frank
Martin, Mr	(E) Mr Knightley's tenant farmer
Mary Bennet	(P & P) Lizzy's sister; plays the piano; reads Fordyce
Crawford	(MP) racy character
King	(P & P) minor character with a lot of money
Maurice and Monty	my inventions
Middleton, Sir John	relative of Mrs Dashwood; provided a cottage
Morlands	(NA) Catharine's loving family
Nabob	a person of conspicuous wealth or high status
Nancy Steele	(S & S) Lucy's sister, a minor character

Norris, Mrs	(MP) harridan sister to the Wards (Lady Bertram, Mrs Price)
Neddy	see Edward Austen-Knight
Odysseus	aka Ulysses—a Greek god of Ithaca
Patrick and Ryan	my inventions
Philadelphia Austen	Mrs Hancock, Jane's aunt
Phillips, Mrs	(P & P) Mrs Bennet's sister
Phil, Usama, Kean	my invention
Price, Lieutenant	(MP) Fanny's father
Frances nee	Ward (MP) Funny's mother, sister to Lady Bertram
Ravenscar	my invention
Robert Ferrars	(S & S) Edward's brother
Ron	my invention
Roper	Thomas Moore's son-in-law
Rosalie	servant to Jane's cousin Eliza
Rowntree	as in chocolate
Rushworths, the	(MP) local gentry
Sally	(N) Sarah Morland sister to Catherine
Steventon	Servant
Samuel Cooke, Rev	Mrs Austen's cousin
Sandra Phillips	(P & P) possible name for Lizzy's cousin
Selina	(E) Mrs Elton's sister
Sidney Parker	(S) dashing brother to Tom
Stanhope, Lady Hester	famous nineteenth-century traveller

Steele, The Misses	(S & S) sisters, supporting characters. See Lucy and Nancy
Stuart	my invention
Susan	Fanny Price's sister
Tattersall	famous reputable horse dealer in $18/19^{th}$ century London.
Theo	could be Theophilus, Mrs Austen's uncle
Thorpe	(NA) family whom Catherine met in Bath
John	(NA) friend of James Morland, Catherine's brother
Tilney, General	(NA) deceived, overbearing father of the Hero
Tom Parker	(S) protagonist entrepreneur
Trevithick, Richard	inventor from Cornwall
Tristan Shandy	author read by Jane Austen
Tysoe Saul Hancock	married Mr Austen's sister Philadelphia in India
Yates, Mr	(MP) minor character, promoter of home theatricals.
Wedgewood	china service, see Jane Austen's House Museum
Wickham	(P & P) deceitful and wicked supporting character
William East, Sir	university friend of Mr Austen's who kept bees

Willoughby	(S & S) protagonist supporting character. A seducer.
Woodhouse, Mr	(E) Emma's father

Topographical Index

Alton	in walking distance from Chawton, Jane's local town
Andover	close enough to the Austens for occasional shopping
Barton Cottage	(S & S) Dashwood's new home in Devon courtesy Sir John
Berlin	Henry Austen was offered a post in Berlin but declined it
Berwick	on-Tweed. A border town between England and Scotland
Birmingham	central to the Industrial Revolution
Bournemouth	seaside town on the south coast
Box Hill	(E) Surrey site of picnic where Emma is unkind to Miss Bates
Brecon Beacons	National Park in South Wales

Bristol	city associated with the Slave Trade during Austen's life
Cardiff	City in South Wales
Carlton House	The Prince Regent's London residence.
Chawton, Hampshire	Jane Austen's last home
Cheltenham	Jane and sister visited this Spa town in Gloucestershire
Cornwall	most south-westerly county in England
Cowes, Isle of wight	Jane may have visited here
Derbyshire Dales	(P & P) Chatsworth House is situated near here.
Donwell Abbey	(S & S) Mr Knightley's home
Gawsworth	village south of Macclesfield, Cheshire
Hampshire	southern county, home of Jane Austen
Highbury	(E) Emma's fictional village in Surrey
Hunsford	(P & P) Where Mr Collins was vicar
Hythe	associated with the docking of ships
Macclesfield	Cheshire, the centre of the silk Industry
Meryton	(P & P) town in walking distance from Bennet's home

Mount Ararat	Turkey. Where some believe Noah landed with his Ark
Netherfield Park	(P & P) rented by Mr Bingley
Oban	Scottish town on the west coast
Purley Hall	Warren Hastings awaited Trial here keeping exotic animals
Richmond, Surrey	(NA) Isabella Thorpe would like a cottage here. (E) Mrs Churchill moves here then dies
River Itchen	Southampton. Jane went rowing on this river with her nephews
Salamanca, Spain	site of Peninsular War infamous battle
Southcliff	my invention
Staffordshire	Midlands County. Hints that Bingley bought a house here
The Lizard	famous tourist spot the most south-westerly tip of England
Truro	cathedral city in south-west Cornwall
Winchester	Hampshire town where Jane Austen died in 1817
Woodston	(NA) Henry Tilney's Living

Abbreviations

J	Juvenilia	MW	Minor Works
S & S	Sense and Sensibility	P & P	Pride and Prejudice
MP	Mansfield Park	E	Emma
P	Persuasion	NA	Northanger Abbey
TW	The Watsons	S	Sanditon
JEAL	James Edward Austen Leigh	HMS	His Majesty's Ship
Berks	Berkshire	Glos	Gloucestershire
Hants	Hampshire	Oxon	Oxfordshire
Staffs	Staffordshire	Warks	Warwickshire
f	fiction	gp	games and puzzles
sp	spin-offs		

References

All references to Jane Austen's letters come from Deidre Le Faye's 3rd edition

Jane Austen's House Museum, Chawton, Hampshire. www.janeaustens.house

Dr Syntax in Search of the Picturesque

Elizabeth Gaskill *North and South* 1854 various publishers
D W Harding *Regulated Hatred and Other Essays* ed M Lawlor. The Athlon Press 1998

J H and E C Hubback *Jane Austen's Sailor Brothers* www.forgottenbooks.org

Elizabeth Jenkins *Jane Austen*

Rudyard Kipling, *Debits and Credits* 1926 Macmillan

Hannah Moore *Caleb in Search of a Wife* Yurita Press 2015

Warren Roberts, *Jane Austen and the French Revolution* 20—
Jon Spence *Becoming Jane*

Flora Thompson 1876-1947 *Lark Rise to Candleford* various
publishers